Investing and Estate Planning Made Easy: Strategies to Make Money and Keep it

Investing and Estate Planning Made Easy: Strategies to Make Money and Keep it

David E. Rosen, Esq.

Copyright © 2016 David E. Rosen, Esq.
All rights reserved.
ISBN: 1530252431
ISBN-13: 9781530252435
Library of Congress Control Number: 2016903589
CreateSpace Independent Publishing Platform
North Charleston, South Carolina

Table of Contents

Introduction

There are known knowns: there are things we know we know. We also know there are known unknowns; that is to say we know there are some things we do not know. But there are also unknown unknowns—the ones we don't know we don't know. And if one looks throughout the history of our country and other free countries, it is the latter category that tend to be the difficult ones.

—DONALD RUMSFELD, FORMER SECRETARY OF DEFENSE

When I heard former Secretary Rumsfeld's comment over a decade ago, I frankly thought it was a ridiculous statement. But the more I thought about it, the more I realized that it made some sense. After all, if you know what information you need, you know what to search for. On the other hand, if you're steeped in darkness, you will blindly search for information that you won't recognize even if you find it.

As Benjamin Franklin wisely observed, "An investment in knowledge pays the best interest." After reading this book, you will understand the process of growing your funds through investment and know what questions to ask your financial advisor. This book will help you make investment decisions, avoid financial mistakes, and figure out whom to trust with your money. The only way to accomplish these goals is by gaining some fundamental financial knowledge.

Most people avoid learning about investments as they believe the information is too esoteric or difficult to understand. It's not; it's really just a matter of learning a new vocabulary and the rules that apply to it. This book will explain the terminology and demystify the rules.

In PART I of this book, I explain

- the rules of investing,
- the types of investment vehicles most investors (including your broker or investment advisor) and individuals use to grow their nest eggs, and
- different strategies for improving your financial position and the potential pitfalls of those strategies.

PART II then explains

- how to keep what you've earned.

Throughout this book, I will focus on five key rules of successful investing:

1. Don't try to time the market.
2. Buy and hold.
3. Diversify broadly.
4. Reduce your costs.
5. Don't buy high and sell low.

These rules cannot be explained in a few words. Each requires some basic understanding of how markets work, the different types of investment vehicles used to increase your money, and a few fundamental principles of economics.

No doubt, you've heard at least some of these rules before. In fact, you are probably thinking, "Easy for you to say, but how?" and "Who are you to advise me on how to grow and protect my money?" Good questions.

I got into investment and estate planning because of personal circumstances that I couldn't have predicted, and it changed the way I viewed my privileged education and my personal goals in life.

I grew up in Worcester, MA and attended Georgetown University Law Center. While living in Washington, D.C., I got a plum job in the social office at the White House. It was a tough place to work, but I got great training. After law school, I worked for Latham & Watkins LLP, a very high-powered law firm and the third largest in the country. Everything was going well until something happened in my family that completely turned around my way of thinking about how I could use my education and training to help people.

My grandmother had a house that she had lived in for fifty years. When she was about ninety years old, her sons (my uncles) heard about the probate process (which I will explain in chapter 12) and decided to take the house out of my grandmother's name and title it in the name of a grandchild. After my grandmother passed away, one of my uncles, who was a bachelor, moved into her house. He met a woman and got married fairly quickly.

About four months after his marriage, my uncle had a bad fall and unexpectedly passed away. Now his new wife, who no one in the family knew very well, was living in my grandmother's home, eating off her china, and insisting that the home now belonged to her. She sued our family; we countersued. The grandchild who held legal title to the house had to represent our family in probate court.

After four expensive years, including trials, appeals, and court and legal fees, the house was returned to our family. But while the legal process ensued, the house fell into disrepair, with each side claiming it was the other party's responsibility to fix it. By this point, the grandchild who had endured all the court battles felt that his experience entitled him to ownership of the house. This started new fights within what used to be a close family. Believe me when I say that holidays together have never been the same.

I have lived the consequences of "do-it-yourself" financial planning; the damage it does to relationships is far worse than any economic loss. This led me to ask myself some difficult questions as I wondered how I could use my legal training to make a difference in people's lives. I was just young enough and stubborn enough to decide to start my own law practice devoted to educating people about how to create estate plans that reflected their personal wishes. This extended into elder law and other issues of retirement planning that I teach in free seminars.

The way I developed my focus on sensible investing was similarly inspired by a personal story. My mother is an intelligent woman, but like most people, did not understand how to invest her money. She did the equivalent of what a lot of people of her generation did and effectively stored it under a mattress. Over time, that money lost its spending power. I wanted to teach her, and people like her, how to manage risk and reward and properly invest their money for growth. Making the right financial decisions for one's unique situation became another subject that I teach in free seminars.

None of us is born knowing how to invest or plan for retirement, and it's not taught in schools. That's why people can be exploited while trying to do the right thing for themselves and their families. No more! This book and my seminars demystify the investment process and will help you understand how to make decisions about growing and protecting your money, or at least give you the questions to ask an investment professional.

Now that you've gotten to know me, let's start understanding how to grow your money and keep as much of it as possible. We'll begin by reviewing what makes some types of investing difficult to distinguish from gambling.

Part I

GROWING YOUR MONEY

One

The Media, Speculation, and Investment Myths

The Hype

When I flip through the channels, I often land on a "financial entertainment" program. Some channels are populated by little else. There's a whole financial entertainment industry built around "experts" screaming advice through television screens. Poised just above streams of numbers whizzing by on the screen, they bark bits of information and opinions at us. They lead us to believe we should watch the Dow like hawks, strike when the market seems hot, and pull out at any sign of trouble.

The volume seems cranked up on these shows, and if you listened for just a minute, you would think you were in the middle of either a rally or a panic.

These shows seem to have four modes (or moods):

1. Euphoria ("The recession is over!" or "All-time high!")
2. Rally ("Don't miss out! This [sector, stock, commodity, etc.] is about to skyrocket!")
3. Dour ("Bears are about to roar!")
4. Panic ("Sell! Sell! Sell!")

To be fair, each of these adjectives does occasionally describe markets appropriately, yet the advice ringing in your ears is rarely helpful.[i] In general, it is best to think of these programs as entertaining rather than informational.

First, it's impossible to get the whole picture from a sound bite. There's too much information out there, and latching onto a single piece of advice is like trying to sip water from a fire hose. In fact, the loudest voice is often contradicted by another "expert" on the same channel.

Second, even if the points you hear are valid, they have almost certainly been factored into market prices by the time you hear them on TV. Remember, ratings are those programs' primary concern—not your nest egg.

Also, as an attorney, I think it's interesting to consider the disclaimers used by the financial media. Here is a lengthy one from *Mad Money*. Read it, and keep it in mind the next time the financial media shouts at you:

All opinions expressed by Jim Cramer on this show are solely Cramer's opinions, and do not reflect the opinions of CNBC, NBC Universal, or their parent company or affiliates, and may have been previously disseminated by Cramer on radio, Internet, or another medium. Cramer's opinions are based upon information he considers reliable, but neither CNBC nor its affiliates or subsidiaries warrant its completeness or accuracy, and it should not be relied upon as such. Cramer's statements and opinions are subject to change without notice. No part of Cramer's compensation from CNBC is related to the specific opinions he expresses. Past performance is not indicative of future results. Neither Cramer nor CNBC guarantees any specific outcome or profit. You should be aware of the real risk of loss in following any strategy or investment discussed on the show.

(This sounds like the disclaimer of so many drug advertisements that include death as one of the possible "side effects.")

Magazines and newspapers are also replete with ads from mutual funds and investment advisors. There's usually a beach, golf course, or yacht in the background. Thousands of funds, advisors, and brokers are competing for your attention. Each wants to lure you in with images of wealth, luxury, and fantasy. When looking at these ads, it's important to remember two things:

1. Through fees, investors are saddled with the costs of these ads.
2. Even the greatest advertisements guarantee nothing.

Speculation

Financial entertainers lead us to believe they're talking about investing. Not so. In reality, they're talking about speculating or trading, which is very different from investing.

The truth is that we can use our knowledge or our gut instinct to make guesses, but that's just a starting point. It's never a guarantee, and it's almost always the first step in a bad decision-making process that results in buying high and selling low.

A popular investment book from the 1990s was Peter Lynch's *Beating the Street*. Lynch advised people to "buy what you know." He described the type of research that should be conducted before investing in a company, but most people just remember the catchphrase without understanding the meaning of "know." The fact that sales are up this month at some company might mean little when balanced against, say, a government investigation or an upcoming earnings revision that you would not know about without doing extensive research.

When someone tells me they're buying into a specific stock, I ask if they've read the latest quarterly report or annual report. Nobody ever answers "yes." If they did, I'd ask if they've read the latest analyst reports and any statements by the CEO or CFO, because there are analysts all over Wall Street who follow business news all day long. It's not that the instincts are necessarily wrong, it's just that there's a lot of information out there and it takes time to consume and digest it all. That makes it nearly impossible to beat the street.

The hard-learned lesson is that gut instinct and hype-based investing can and often will crush your finances. At the end of this process, people are frustrated and tired of speculating; they often want out of the stock market altogether. The silver lining is that they are now in the ideal mental state to forget what they heard on CNBC, ignore the tip from their cousin, and learn about real investing.

But first, let's dispel some of the biggest myths perpetuated by the financial entertainment industry.

Investment Myths

When someone steps into my office for the first time, they usually have questions based on something they heard on CNBC or FOX Business Network. I find myself dispelling the myriad myths perpetuated by the financial entertainment industry that keep people investing with particular funds or firms. These myths, like other fictions, become pervasive and resilient. Did you know that Thomas Edison did *not* invent the light bulb?[ii] (Numerous people contributed to its invention, but Thomas Edison, already a well-known inventor, was also a great self-promoter.) That's a harmless myth (though it probably didn't feel harmless to the other inventors). Other investment myths are far more insidious and damaging. Learning the truth behind the most prominent myths will help you to make knowledgeable, well-informed decisions for your portfolio.[iii]

Financial Benchmarks

Let's start with basic financial benchmarks. Understanding them will help you understand the stock market as well as financial advertising and the myths that permeate it.

> **DEFINITION FINANCIAL BENCHMARK: a standard against which the performance of a stock, bond, mutual fund, or any other financial instrument can be measured**

In the financial world, there are dozens of indices that analysts use to evaluate performance.

For example, the performance of a financial manager for a mutual fund that invests in tech stocks can be compared against the NASDAQ Composite Index, a collection of four thousand technology-oriented stocks. This index fund examines the technology sector of the economy as a whole, including tech stocks that are performing well or performing poorly.

You can use many variables to define an index: market sector, market capitalization, and so on. The more individual stocks and sectors encompassed by an index, the "broader" it is relative to other indices. A broader index is less susceptible to sudden shocks to a particular stock or sector. That holds true for booms and busts alike, since the risks are spread across a wider range of investments. The broadest indices are best for viewing the market as a whole. That's why they serve as benchmarks for comparison. Here are the most popular US stock market indices:

- **Dow Jones Industrial Average (Dow Jones)**: A price-weighted index of thirty of the largest US corporations.
- **S&P 500 (Standard and Poor's 500)**: A market-capitalization-weighted stock index based on the market capitalizations of five

hundred leading companies, as determined by Standard and Poor's, that are publicly traded in the US stock markets.

- **Wilshire 5000**: This index aims to track the returns of virtually all publicly traded, US-based stocks that trade on the major exchanges. Like the S&P 500, the Wilshire 5000 is market-capitalization-weighted, so larger companies have more influence on the index's movements.

Of course, you shouldn't stop at comparing past performance to a financial benchmark; there's more to consider before assuming that a stock, mutual fund or financial manager is a trustworthy investment. Keep this in mind as we turn to the big investment myths.

Myth Number 1: Stock Picking

The myth: Investment advisors can consistently add value to your portfolio by exercising superior skill in individual stock selection.

The truth: Regardless of how intelligent or talented a financial advisor is, past ability to pick stocks has little or no correlation with his or her ability to repeat stock-picking success in the future.

Here's a question I get all the time: "Hey, David, what do you think about [insert company name]?" Usually, they are excited about a company or product they've just read about (or, more likely, heard about on TV) and have come to believe this certain company's stock is a sure bet. They want me to confirm their instinct to invest. I understand the desire to get in on something early and strike it rich, but I never recommend individual stocks. I recommend that they don't take the bait, because the likelihood of it working out the way they expect is miniscule. Unfortunately, the fact is that the financial media preys on this desire on both the micro (individual stock) and macro (mutual fund) levels.

In fact, the most prominent investment philosophy in the financial world is based on the idea that financial markets don't properly price individual stocks. Some investment firms convince clients they have the ability to consistently predict the future. You may have heard an advisor say something like, "This stock is the new Apple!" to entice buyers to invest in a low-priced stock that they believe will skyrocket. By buying these allegedly mispriced stocks, they suggest that you can profit from the new price when the market corrects itself.

On the surface, it seems to make sense that these advisors can really predict stock values. We see advertisements for mutual funds that earned 10 percent over the S&P 500 during the past two to five years, or who will be the next big fund manager, or what will be the "hottest" new stock. Financial firms with advertising power appear trustworthy because they employ some of the brightest and most financially savvy minds in the world, from MIT mathematicians to Harvard MBAs. John Bogle, founder of the Vanguard Group, advises investors or even fund managers to avoid picking stocks, because each pick carries its own type of unnecessary risk.

The truth is that most mutual funds earn less over a five-year period than a benchmark index, such as the S&P 500. If managers were truly able to identify mispriced stocks, bonds, and other financial instruments, then the majority of mutual funds would offer better returns than a benchmark index. Yet more often than not, fund managers are unable to beat the market.[iv] Even the handful of actively managed funds that do outperform the S&P 500 index can't demonstrate that their active management was the reason for the fund's superior performance. The fact is that fund performance is overwhelmingly indistinguishable from luck. Of course, the fact that taking credit for fund performance is like taking credit for an eclipse doesn't stop fund managers from touting their track record to lure investors.

To be sure, stock picking can be tempting. That's especially so when we fall behind on our savings goals and feel pressured to make up for lost time. That situation prompts many people to seek a home-run investment. For some people, stock picking is fun—while they're ahead.[v] But it's stressful to be wrong. Even if you're right in week one or quarter one, you have to continuously do your homework or else you're just gambling. Remember: when it comes to gambling, the house (casino) *always* eventually wins. If you've got money to burn, that's one thing. But don't pretend you're doing anything other than gambling. And before you pull the trigger, think about all the other, more interesting things you can do with your spare money besides gambling.

A friend of mine invested in a few stocks based mostly on watching CNBC after he landed a big law-firm job. That was in mid-2008. He was ahead 20 percent in two weeks. But less than two weeks later, he was down 60 percent due to the market crash. At that point, his wife told him to just hold onto the shares and see if they recovered. Instead, he panicked and sold near the bottom. A year or so later, when the market rebounded, he had missed out yet again. Not only had the market recovered, but it also had risen. My friend had sold his Apple shares at around $25, and as I write this, Apple shares are trading around $125.

> **KEY PRINCIPLE: *Over time, the stock market tends to transfer money from greedy and fearful speculators to vigilant and rational investors.***

No matter what you see on TV, speculation is *not* investing. If you're going to listen to financial media, you must develop a mental filter that separates speculation from wise investing. Ask yourself whether the investment fits into your overall plan. If you are committed to a plan that is properly tailored to your needs, stick with it! If the investment will take you off track, it's probably a mistake.

To immunize yourself from the myth, remember that *nobody* knows what stocks are going to go up next week—not your cousin, not your broker, not your advisor. Over time, the performance of 99.9 percent of stock pickers is indistinguishable from luck. That's why I advise investors not to try to time the market. Keep this point in mind while you consider the next big myth.

Myth Number 2: Market Timing

The myth: Money managers are able to utilize market timing to predict when markets will rise and fall.

The truth: It's virtually impossible for even the most experienced traders to consistently jump in and out just in time to catch the best days and avoid the worst days.

A stock's price is based on the earning potential of the company that issued shares. The way the market views a company's earning potential depends upon several factors, including the company's ability to earn profits, the state of the company's sector, and changes in the economy.

Money managers who rely on market timing look at the various economic indicators and try to guess how the market is going to react to new information. They also try to predict exactly what that information is going to be (employment statistics, inflation, interest rates, currency exchange rates, commodity prices, etc.). They believe that by predicting how the market will react, they can buy or sell before the market rises or falls.

INVESTMENT RULE 1: Don't Try to Time the Market

But market timing doesn't work as an investment strategy. When news is made public, the market almost immediately analyzes the effects it may have on a particular company, and the share price changes accordingly.

Unless the fund manager finds out about the news announcement before everyone else (which is known as "insider information"), he will get the information at the same time as everyone else. I can't overemphasize this point.

The High Cost of Bad Timing

Missing the market's top-performing days can prove costly to a portfolio's worth. Let's consider an investor who missed *only* the ten top-performing days during the twenty-year period from 1993 to 2012. That's ten out of 5,040 trading days. That investor who was out of the market for those 10 days would have earned *half* as much as an investor who remained in the market for the entire period.[vi] They would have left fifty percent of their potential gains on the table by missing ten days out of twenty *years*. Constantly buying and selling not only has its own costs (commissions on transaction costs), but there are also risks of missing out when an investment begins to move up again. The same thing is true on the downside, but over time, the market has consistently risen, so the opportunity cost on the upside exceeds the downside in the long run.

Let's consider an example. Let's say Irving the Investor put $10,000 into his portfolio. If he held that investment for that same twenty-year time period (1993–2002), it would have been worth $44,087. But another investor who missed the ten top-performing days during that period would have only $22,050 to show for it—still a gain, but only half as much as Irving's investment was worth *and* less than he could have earned via a safer investment in T-Bills. When it comes to long-term wealth, being out of the market can be very expensive.

INVESTMENT RULE 2: Buy and Hold

Nobody can move your money in and out of the markets at precisely the right time over an extended period. For a market-timing approach to succeed, you have to be correct twice—first, when you leave the stock market, and second, when you jump back in.[vii] The best we can do is spread our risk (by investing broadly) and hedge our bets (by diversification).

It's tempting to believe there's someone out there who can rescue us from uncertainty—someone with sophisticated algorithms or a brilliant research staff. There isn't. Nobody knows what the next decade, year, month, or even week will look like in the stock market. You should run from any advisor who tells you he can. Sure, experts can model the direction of the economy based on historical data, but as we learn every time a bubble bursts or the market crashes, those experts are often wrong. By accepting that nobody knows exactly how stock prices are going to behave, we can let go of some of the anxiety of speculation, and turn our focus to responsible investing.

Efficient Markets

The efficient-market hypothesis[viii] states that it is impossible for anyone (without inside information) to predict outcomes in the market, because share prices always reflect all known information. Although analysts who follow different industries and companies are paid to have the most up-to-date information and insight into the unique circumstances affecting the companies they follow, it is unlikely for anyone to be able to invest in a significantly undervalued stock or be able to sell a significantly overvalued stock. People who make these predictions are making educated guesses that may pay off, but they are still guesses. Beware of anyone who contends that he knows what the market or any investment will do over a given period of time.

Myth Number 3: Chasing Last Year's Winners

The myth: Working with funds or financial managers that did well in the past is a good method of indicating which funds or managers will do well in the future.

The truth: Past performance is no guarantee of future success.

One of the first things most people do before investing is look at a fund's (or firm's) record of accomplishment, aiming to find ones with a record of returns that beat a financial benchmark. In fact, the funds and firms depend on people doing so. Unfortunately, the disclaimer you've heard is true: "Past performance does not guarantee future results." There's no evidence of a long-term correlation. None. (We'll discuss this further in chapter 3.)

Myth Number 4: Superior Performance Justifies Higher Fees

The myth: High costs are offset by superior performance.

The truth: A lot of buying and selling happens in the mutual fund investment process, incurring hidden costs that reduce your gains.

Theoretically, a fund could provide such superior returns that you'd benefit even if it charged more in fees. Lots of funds (and firms) would like you to believe that their performance justifies their fees. They rarely do, though it's not always easy to tell exactly how much you are losing to fees or other trading costs.

Funds incur costs beyond just the management fees they charge. Even funds with low management fees incur hidden costs that appear only in the fine print. Whenever a fund manager buys or sells a stock, the fund pays for that transaction.

Myth Number 5: Playing It Safe

The myth: We can accumulate enough for retirement by saving cash and buying cash equivalents.

The truth: Inflation robs cash, CDs and T-Bills of their purchasing power.

In 2014, a savings account typically paid 0.1 percent in interest. CDs paid 0.7 percent. Inflation was a "modest" 1.7 percent. The money in a typical savings account or CD actually *lost* between 1 percent and 1.6 percent in purchasing power.

Let's say you sock away $100,000 in cash for retirement, and inflation returns to 3 percent—the historical annual rate of inflation. That $100,000 effectively dwindles to $75,409.39 of purchasing power in ten years, $55,367.58 in twenty years, $41,198.68 in thirty years, and $30,655.68 in forty years. Most people hope to spend twenty, twenty-five, or thirty years—or even longer—in retirement. By "playing it safe" and putting your savings into CDs or T-Bills and so on, you're allowing inflation to devour your retirement plans.

I hope this chapter has inoculated you against the dangerous investment myths that the financial industry perpetuates. By creating a plan that works for you and casting a wide net with your investments, you will avoid most of the pitfalls associated with these myths. As Dan Solin, best-selling author of *The Smartest...* series of investment and retirement-planning books says, investors should be focused on asset allocation. You should avoid actively managed funds and ignore all advice about market timing and stock selection. In short, you should follow responsible principles of investing. That means creating an investment plan with your financial advisor, developing Zen-like confidence in your plan, and sticking to it, even when financial experts and the media try to entice you into jumping ship and following a glittery new trend.

With this understanding, we can now lay the foundation for your investing success.

Summary

- Don't buy into the hype or panic of the market and make emotional investment decisions.
- Understand the difference between gambling and investing.
- Financial benchmarks allow us to measure our investments against a standard.
- Over time, the stock market rewards rational investors.
- It is not possible to time the market and get in and out at the right moment.
- Markets are efficient—all known information is reflected in the price.
- Playing it safe with your investments will not allow you to earn more than the rate of inflation.

Two

Laying the Groundwork for Success: Fundamental Concepts

Risk versus Return

No discussion of investments can take place without an understanding of the fundamental concept of risk. Investments that are high risk can provide a high reward or may end up losing much of their value. An aggressive, risk-loving investor who doesn't need the money in the near term may invest in riskier, more volatile assets. This approach is appropriate for someone with high earning potential who doesn't expect to need the cash soon, for example, to purchase a house.

> **DEFINITION RISK TOLERANCE: your individual willingness to lose some or all of your investment capital in exchange for larger potential returns**

An investor closer to retirement age probably has a lower tolerance for risk than the high-wage earner and will likely favor a conservative investment approach to preserve capital. For this investor, a lower-risk portfolio that produces more modest returns is appropriate, as it doesn't expose the investment to the risk of losing value just when he is ready to retire.

Each investment strategy, however, also needs to be weighed relative to the tax implications of the investment. A high-wage earner may be in a high tax bracket, which means that his capital gains will be more heavily taxed than those of someone in a lower tax bracket. Make sure your investment advisor is knowledgeable both about a range of investment strategies and their tax consequences to help you keep as much as possible of what you gain. (For a fuller discussion of the tax implications of different investments, see chapter 13.)

> *KEY PRINCIPLE: Choose your investment professional with as much care as you choose a primary doctor. You must feel comfortable being completely honest with the person you delegate to invest your money.*

Every investor has a different risk profile, and your investment advisor, in consultation with you, should choose one that fits your unique needs and circumstances. Be sure to let your investment advisor know your important upcoming plans (such as retirement or a home purchase) as well as concerns (such as health and healthcare costs).

How to Look at Performance Gains and Losses

When the market value of investments declines, it's natural to experience a fear of falling short of your goals. Understanding loss, relative loss, and relative gains can help alleviate such fears.

- **Loss:** performance loss occurs when a portfolio's value decreases due to changing market conditions or a fall in a company's earnings.

There are, however, more nuanced ways of understanding losses.

- **Relative loss:** Any fund's performance can be compared *relative to a benchmark index*. This is a measure of opportunity cost relative to an index like the S&P 500. When an investor experiences a relative loss, the investment may increase in value but rise less than it would have if he or she had invested in the benchmark itself.

> **DEFINITION** S&P 500 INDEX: The S&P 500 is a U.S. stock market index based on the market capitalization of 500 large companies listed on the New York Stock Exchange (NYSE) or NASDAQ.[ix] It is a representation of the U.S. stock market.

For example, imagine that you invested in a mutual fund whose price increases 3 percent by year-end. Even though the fund's value has increased, you might still experience a relative loss if the S&P increased by 10 percent during that same time period.

> **DEFINITION** OPPORTUNITY COST: a determination of gain forgone when funds are used for an alternate purpose. For example, the cost of attending business school is not only the expense of tuition, but also the salary not earned during that two-year period.

- **Relative gain:** On the other hand, you can lose money in a fund but still have a relative gain if your own investments lose less than the benchmark index. If your funds lost 2 percent of their value but the S&P lost 5 percent of its value, you would have had a relative gain, even if your investment declined in value since you lost less than the benchmark.

Inflation

Another important factor to consider in the context of your investments is the role of inflation.

In June 1975, when Steve Jobs and Steve Wozniak invented the Apple computer,[ix] actual apples cost around $0.34 per pound. In September 2015, apples cost approximately $1.30 per pound—a 382 percent increase. That's a fairly typical example of inflation, which, over the past forty years, has cumulatively totaled 343 percent. This means that if you had kept money under your mattress from 1975 to 2015, you would have experienced a loss of buying power of 343 percent.

Since the 2008 financial meltdown, Americans have benefited from a relatively low rate of inflation—approximately 1.5 percent per year. However, considering the vast quantity of money printed (known as "quantitative easing") by the federal government since 2008, it is inevitable that inflation will make a resounding and most unwelcome return. Historically, assuming a 3 percent annual rate of inflation has been a good rule of thumb. Your investment advisor should strive to provide returns that exceed the benchmark index as well as the rate of inflation. That's why stuffing money under your mattress is a poor financial strategy. Even if you don't touch it, you're losing approximately 3 percent in spending power every year.

Back when savings-account-interest rates were above 3 percent, banks could at least protect your nest egg from inflation. But since 2008, the Federal Reserve has kept interest rates artificially low; the average savings account now pays interest at an annual rate south of 0.2 percent—only nominally higher than your mattress. That's why even the most risk-averse investor has to be well informed about financial planning in general and retirement planning in particular.

Diversification

You've heard the sage advice, "Don't put all your eggs in one basket." That's diversification. The S&P 500 is an index based on the market capitalizations of five hundred large companies having common stock listed on the New York Stock Exchange (NYSE) or NASDAQ. It is far more likely that one of those companies will go bankrupt in any given year than it is that one hundred of them will. Each individual company has its own risks, and most companies can be accurately categorized into one of several different economic sectors—for example, technology, banking, or mining—each of which is associated with different risks or cyclical trends.

By investing in only a few companies, you remain largely exposed to the "unsystematic" risks (which affect only an industry or a specific company) that each one faces. Conversely, by investing in a pool of different stocks, you lower the risk of a few bad apples wiping you out completely. You will also realize the additional benefit of reducing the overall volatility of your portfolio, considering that losses in a diversified portfolio are often offset by gains and vice versa.

What you're betting on is that the combined change in value of all of your shares taken together will, over time, make you money. Historically, that's been a safe bet. But over a long period, there will certainly be times when you're down across the board. Understandably, those are tough times, but I will repeatedly tell you that the wisest course of action during those times is to wait and ride out the storm.

Diversifying is Investing 101, but it's easier said than done. Most individual investors lack sufficient resources to effectively diversify on their own. If you wanted to buy shares of five hundred different publicly traded companies, you'd need over $2 million and would incur prohibitive transaction costs. And your basket *still* would not include small-value stocks, international stocks, or bonds.

INVESTMENT RULE 3: Diversify Broadly

So Wall Street devised "commingled investment vehicles" that enable multiple investors to pool their assets to spread out their individual risk. Mutual funds, variable annuity subaccounts, and exchange-traded funds (ETFs) are examples of such vehicles. These vehicles achieve greater diversification, allowing individual investors to invest simultaneously in thousands of different stocks, with each investor owning a proportional share of those assets. By pooling assets with other investors, we achieve a far higher degree of diversification than we can alone. In chapter 6, you will learn about the most common type of commingled investment: the mutual fund.

Summary

- Determine your level of risk tolerance based on your unique circumstances and your time horizon for investing.
- Share your goals and concerns honestly with your financial advisor so that he can devise a portfolio that will meet your personal goals.
- Understand the differences between absolute and relative performance gain and loss that compare your results to the performance of a benchmark index.
- Investment strategies should try to ensure that your portfolio's buying power increases relative to the rate of inflation.
- Diversify broadly to spread your risk and avoid the type of risk that affects only a particular industry or company.

Three

A successful investment strategy requires understanding more than the technical factors involved in growing your investment. It also requires understanding the very real role that emotion plays—not only on an investor but also on an investment professional.

For example, a rational person knows that inflation (and, in recent history, abnormally low interest rates) makes putting money into a savings account with 0.1 percent interest or hiding it under his or her mattress a poor strategy for maintaining or growing purchasing power. But the overwhelming amount of information that investors confront causes great uncertainty, much like the feeling of being a rat lost in a maze. Understanding a little about investor psychology will help you navigate that maze and enjoy the satisfying taste of the cheese when you reach your goal.

Dalbar QAIB (1984-2013) Results Summary[xi]	
Category	1984-2013 Annualized Return
S&P 500 Index	11.10%
Average Investor	3.69%
Inflation	2.80%

According to Dalbar Inc., a firm that studies investor behavior, between 1984 and 2013, the S&P 500 index earned, on average, 11.10 percent each year. Over the same period, the average investor earned an average of only 3.69 percent each year.[x] That is only 0.89 percent above the rate of inflation and far short of the S&P 500's performance by a staggering of 7.41 percent! How is that possible?

While someone who invested $10,000 in the S&P 500 in 1984 could have earned $225,000 during that same period, that person left, on average, 67 percent of the potential gain ($150,750) on the table. That money went, instead, to the brokerage firms through commissions and fees.

KEY PRINCIPLE: *Turnover and transaction costs (buying and selling stocks) eat up 67 percent of an investor's potential gain.*

According to Dalbar president Lou Harvey, individual investors typically mistime their trading decisions: they do the wrong thing at the wrong time, even though their money depends on them getting in and out of an investment at the right time. Such poor timing can often be traced to a counterproductive cycle known as the "investor's dilemma" that many people go through when making investment decisions. This involves making decisions based on emotions rather than on facts. Understanding and recognizing this cycle is the best way to ensure that you avoid it altogether.

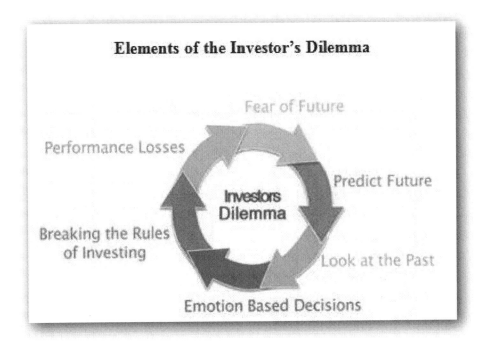

Dangerous Emotions

Investors typically fear not having enough money to live comfortably when they retire or becoming a burden to family and friends in their old age. They also have a fear of investing poorly, a fear of missing out on a golden opportunity, and a fear of not being able to interpret complex information. While fear drives many hasty decisions, it is not the only dangerous emotion. Excitement also leads people to make hasty decisions. People get excited about the prospect of getting rich, imagining they are getting in on the "ground floor" of the next big investment boom.

The investment industry exploits these emotions in its advertising, using past fund performance to attract investment in their fund. By implying that they can predict the market's future, investment firms prey on investors' emotions.

> **DEFINITION PROBABILITY THEORY**: the analysis of random phenomena. It is not possible to predict the outcome of discrete events.[xiii]

Reliance on Past Performance

What's wrong with relying on past performance? Isn't that the best indication of future performance?

According to the law of probability, a fund has a 50 percent chance of increasing in any year and a 50 percent chance of decreasing over the same time period. The fact that it increases one year does not change the fact that the following year it still has a fifty-fifty chance of increasing or decreasing.

In addition, the information provided about a fund's returns are not the whole story. Brokerages may have hundreds or thousands of mutual funds that contain different mixes of the asset classes. By random chance, some will do well, while others will not. What these funds advertise, but don't explain, is that *one* of their funds achieved the "past performance" results that they promote. They don't mention that all their other funds fell short of that level of performance. When you're looking at past performance, remember that you're only seeing part of the picture.

This is like misinterpreting the sign posted in casinos that reads, "We Pay Back 92 Percent of Your Money!" (The exclamation mark is intended to make you believe that this is a good thing.) And 92 percent out of 100 is good—until you realize that it means that, on average, the *best* a gambler can hope to do is lose only 8 percent of his money. (Some people will win more than this average, and some people will lose more.) Expecting a fund to achieve the same performance as it did the previous year is just gambling with your investment.

Mutual funds, retail brokers, and financial advisors aggressively market funds awarded four and five stars by Morningstar, the Chicago-based arbiter of investment performance. But the rating system merely identifies funds that performed well in the past; it provides no help in finding future winners. The search for top-performing stock funds is an exercise that will come to be viewed as one of the great financial follies of the late twentieth century.

Here's an example of performance-based marketing. In the November 2000 issue of *Money* magazine, there was an ad headline: "Tech Stocks Still Hot." It touted a number-one ranking and five stars. In 1998, the fund returned 196 percent, and 216 percent in 1999! Pretty impressive, right? But if you added this fund to your portfolio in 1999 or 2000, you would have noticed that it returned a dismal –0.51 percent in 2000. I'm quite sure there were no similar ads for the fund in 2001.

As the chart below illustrates, the reality is that even the top funds rarely exhibit the same performance for even *two* consecutive years.

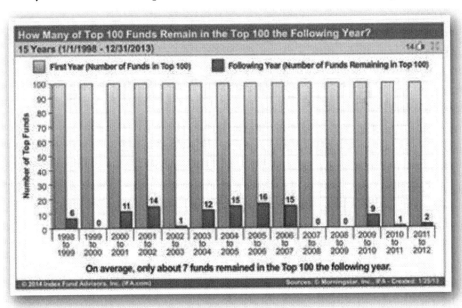

From 2002 to 2012, on average only 7 percent of the Top-100 fund managers repeated their performance the following year. In the years 2008 and 2009, *no* fund managers repeated their previous year's Top-100 performance.

Funds focus on "past performance" for one simple reason: because it works in attracting new investment. A *Wall Street Journal* and Morningstar study found that 72 percent of consumers invested their money in four- and five-star-rated mutual funds that showed the highest returns during the previous three to five years.[xi]

To understand what's going on here, you simply have to look at the law of large numbers.

Mutual Funds and the Law of Large Numbers

One way mutual fund managers achieve a four- to five-star rating is by taking advantage of the law of large numbers. A manager who actively or passively manages a large number of mutual funds has a very high chance of obtaining one or more funds that outperform the stock market across the two-, three-, or five-year period that is used to determine a mutual fund's rating. If you only have one mutual fund, then the chance that that fund will outperform the market for five years in a row is very small. However, if you have one hundred mutual funds, the chance that at least one will outperform the market is higher. All a mutual fund manager needs to do is create enough funds to increase the statistical likelihood that at least one will beat the market for five straight years and then aggressively publicize that fund's performance. By dissolving the unsuccessful funds and pointing to the successful fund(s), a fund manager can profit handsomely from *pretending* to know what the future holds.

Information Overload and Emotional Decision Making

There are over ten thousand publicly traded stocks and thirty thousand mutual funds. How can anyone possibly know which are good or bad investments? How can you determine what factors will positively or negatively affect those investments?

We are constantly bombarded with information, performance statistics, and marketing messages about investment options. Every firm tries to convince us that they are the best, but their products are virtually indistinguishable from those of their competitors. In the face of so much information and distractions, people understandably resort to making investment decisions based on emotion rather than logic.

KEY PRINCIPLE: Successful investing is about behavior,
not skill.

Whenever emotions drive decisions, we make bad choices. Individual investors tend to act hastily, selling a stock whose price is falling or buying one from a company that someone says is "hot." Even experienced fund managers act on emotion, trading stocks in their portfolios far more often than necessary. (We'll discuss this problem in chapter 5).

Bad for You, Good for Brokers

Acting on emotion tends to benefit the investment industry while being detrimental to investors. Remember, in addition to a potential opportunity cost, every trade you make triggers a fee or commission. For that reason, brokers have little incentive to discourage your trading decisions.

> **DEFINITION** **TRANSACTION COST**: fees or commissions paid when buying or selling an investment

This holds true for fund managers as well as individual investors. In the case of a mutual fund, the fund pays commissions, and possibly other fees, that are deducted from your portfolio. (There's even a form of fraud called "churning," which is when brokers execute pointless or unnecessary trades to generate more commissions. That's why it's important to understand how your investment professional is compensated, as discussed in chapter 8.)

Recognizing the Emotional Cycle

The chart below illustrates the emotional roller coaster underlying the investor's dilemma.[xii] If investors' account balances increase, they tend to be happy; if their account balances decrease, they tend to be unhappy. When an investor lacks confidence, he may be driven to sell low and make other unwise changes to his portfolio. Most investors don't realize when they're caught in this cycle.

Similarly, when a fund manager's predictions about the market prove incorrect, he may lose confidence in his decisions and make unnecessary changes in his clients' portfolios. Although these changes may be motivated by a desire to protect the investor, making hasty changes breaks one of the key rules of sound investing and almost invariably results in lower returns.

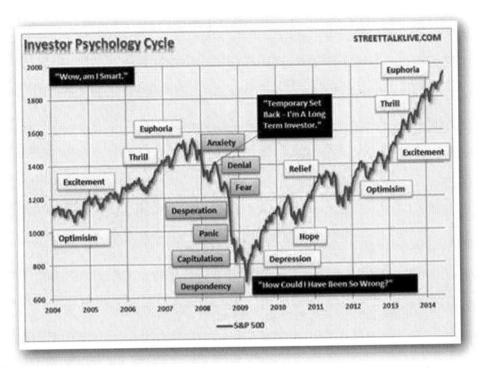

The desire to limit losses is a perfectly reasonable, but it brings the investor back to the beginning of the cycle, which begins with fear. If that fear had led an investor to cash out early in 2009, he would have missed the mid-2009 rally. That's why "buy and hold" is one of the key rules of investing.

Breaking the Cycle

As explained in chapter 3, inflation eats away at money languishing in a bank or under a mattress. The fear of making a mistake rightly makes us pause before sinking our savings into an investment vehicle.

We are emotional beings, and often need to make important decisions based on limited information. Since this will never change, errors are inevitable; they should be acknowledged, learned from, and planned for. As George Soros, a highly successful investor, correctly observed,

"Once we realize that imperfect understanding is the human condition, there is no shame in being wrong, only failing to correct our mistakes."

Being very specific and clear about your goals when creating your financial plan is an effective way to minimize errors. A well-organized, comprehensive, and specific financial plan will help avoid the temptation to cash out when you hear colleagues talking about taking expensive vacations, buying a new car, and so on. It also helps to remember what you're risking before you decide to shift into more volatile investments. Being honest with yourself and a trusted advisor at the planning stage will give you greater confidence in your plan—confidence that, in turn, will spare you from many sleepless nights and premature gray hair.

Here is some sage wisdom that I have found particularly helpful:

- Have *realistic* expectations about the future.
- Let go of outcomes we can't control.
- Do second-guess; trust your plan.
- Don't measure yourself against others.

Moving Forward

After experiencing the highs and lows of the Investor Psychology Cycle, people tend to become frustrated and tired of speculation. The silver lining is that they've reached an excellent mental state to learn about real investing. Simply stated, the most effective way to escape (or avoid) the investor's dilemma is to become an informed investor. If you have a basic understanding of what you're doing, why you're doing it, what the costs are, and what to expect, you will feel a greater sense of comfort and confidence. Without that confidence, you'll likely be driven to make changes that end up costing money and peace of mind. With knowledge, guidance, and an informed investment strategy, you'll improve your chances of meeting or exceeding your retirement goals.

So how can you build a retirement portfolio that protects and grows your savings so you can use your hard-earned money in your golden years? Develop, with the guidance of your investment professional, a plan that considers your unique issues, and stick to it. Chapter 10 will help you do just that.

Summary

- Recognize and avoid the investor's dilemma.
- Past performance of a mutual fund is no indication of projected future performance.
- Acting on emotion is dangerous if for no other reason than frequent trading results in transaction costs.

Four

TYPES OF ASSETS AND THEIR ROLES IN YOUR PORTFOLIO

In his famous book, *A Random Walk Down Wall Street*, Burton Malkiel said, "A blindfolded monkey throwing darts at a newspaper's financial pages could select a portfolio that would do just as well as one carefully selected by experts." In 2012, Research Affiliates of Newport Beach, CA, actually tested this theory and found that the monkeys *beat* the index by an average of 1.7 percent for every year since 1964.[xiii] How, then, can any investor hope to figure out how to sensibly choose an investment strategy?

The first factor to understand is the nature of the investment options available to you. The following list does not include every investment vehicle available, but reviews the major ones that are likely to comprise your portfolio.

Understanding Asset Classes

Each asset class theoretically has the same overall goal—to make money over time—yet each serves a different function in terms of risk and reward.

> **DEFINITION ASSET:** an economic resource. Assets can be tangible (like cash, inventory, or equipment) or intangible (like copyrights, patents, stocks, and bonds).[xvii]

The following asset classes are listed from the lowest- to the highest-risk investments:

Treasury bills: Treasury Bills, or T-Bills, are the instruments the US government uses to borrow money for less than one year. Safety is the key function of T-Bills, because they have never gone down in value. These days, however, T-Bills don't go up much in value, either. Since they mature in less than one year, the risk of interest-rate changes is minimal. Depending on how you calculate it, the rate of return is typically around 0.9 percent above the rate of inflation. That's not much of a return, but that's not the purpose of T-Bills; the purpose is safety. If your risk tolerance is low (e.g., upon retirement), it is appropriate to move more of your money into this asset class.

Long-term treasury bonds: T-Bonds provide a slight increase in return in exchange for a longer maturity period—typically ten to thirty years. In December 2015, the T-Bond rate was 4.615 percent. In December 2001, the rate was 8.283 percent. Over the past thirty years, the interest rate for T-Bonds has remained roughly in the range of 3 to 9 percent.

Bonds are in your portfolio to provide safety. Long-term bonds tend to go up when the stock market goes down because of what is called a "flight to quality." When people panic, they buy what they believe is stable and safe: US government bonds. Why? The government can tax and print money and will not go bankrupt. Investors can feel comfortable that they will get their money back. As the demand for bonds goes up, so does their value. But they still carry some risk.

Between the 1920s and the 1980s, interest rates rose, but ever since then they have declined. In 2009, the trading value of T-Bonds dropped an average of 14.9 percent. Indeed, from 2010 through 2015, short-term interest rates were at the lowest possible rate—0.25 percent—with two-year bonds also returning less than 1 percent during this period. Although T-Bonds recently received a nominal bump up to 0.5 percent, current interest rates remain essentially at sixty-year lows.

In 2002, when the stock market went down 22 percent, intermediate-term bonds (those maturing in three to ten years) experienced a 16 percent return. That's even better than it looks, because these intermediate-term bonds went *up* 16 percent up when large US stocks went *down* 22 percent. In 2008, when large US stocks went down around 40 percent, intermediate-term bonds rose 13 percent. That is the purpose of bonds in your portfolio: they provide safety just when you need it most.

Large stocks, US and international: Large US stocks make up a disproportionate share of Americans' portfolios. That is partly for marketing reasons and partly because people tend to invest in what is familiar or what they hear about. People are often surprised to learn that large US stocks went through two twenty-year periods during the last century when they offered *no returns* after inflation (1929 to the mid-1950s, and 1966 to 1982). Even if these stocks feel like a safe bet, it's risky to have all of your money in this area of the market.

From 1973 to 2013, the annualized return on large US stocks was 10.27 percent. Large international stocks' annualized return was 9.51 percent. The returns are very similar in the long run, but most people feel more comfortable investing in US companies, without realizing that large corporations sometimes change their citizenship. For example, Anheuser-Busch, the largest brewery in the United States, has been headquartered in Belgium since InBev acquired it in 2008. Similarly, in

2015, US pharmaceutical giant Pfizer announced plans to merge into Allergan, an Irish company.

The point is that globalization of industry has eliminated some of the distinctions between domestic and foreign-based corporations. We don't think very differently about Hershey chocolate in the United States versus Nestlé chocolate in Switzerland. They're both big, well-known publicly traded companies in a competitive market. And over time, both US and international large stocks tend to provide higher returns than bonds. Of course, with that higher return also comes a higher degree of volatility—in other words, risk.

Small stocks, US and international: We see similar performance in small US stocks and small international stocks. (Their names will likely be unfamiliar to you. The Russell 2000 is the benchmark index for small US stocks. The portion of the portfolio focused on these stocks aims to match the returns of the Russell 2000.) Over a thirty-year period, small US stocks and small international stocks have had similar returns: 12.92 percent and 13.39 percent, respectively. While you might think small international stocks would carry a much higher risk than small US stocks, the research shows that adding this asset class to a portfolio actually *reduces* overall risk, because circumstances affecting stocks in the United States are usually not the same circumstances affecting international stocks. In late 2001 and early 2002, small international stocks were the ones that resisted the market downturn that affected the United States.

Value stocks, US and international: Value stocks are shares of companies that have lower market prices than comparable companies of a similar size.[xiv] This is usually due to lower-than-expected earnings and/or some underlying distress. As a result, they are a riskier investment, but they carry the potential for some of the highest returns if the company is able to right the ship.

On Balance

Remember our dart-throwing monkeys? The reason that a random approach to picking stocks was more successful than a deliberate one was that monkeys don't care about market capitalization. Their darts were not aimed at or hitting only the largest companies. They also hit smaller companies whose share prices experienced higher growth over time than many of the larger ones.

A well-balanced portfolio may allocate a portion of the total investment to each of the above asset classes in different proportions. In general, we expect greater returns for stocks over bonds, small companies over large companies, and value companies over growth companies. The challenge for your investment advisor is to use this knowledge to optimize your investments.

> **KEY PRINCIPLE: *You will typically make more money from stocks than from bonds.***

But asset class is not the only basis of the investment decision. Another important factor to consider is your time horizon. The more time you have, the more risk you may be comfortable taking on, since you can wait out economic cycles and downturns. In contrast, if you expect to need the money within five years—for example, to finance a child's college education—the shorter time horizon would make less risky investments more appropriate.

> **DEFINITION TIME HORIZON:** the anticipated amount of time you expect to invest in order to achieve a specific goal

Summary

- Balance your portfolio's risks and rewards through asset allocation to different asset classes.
- The choice of asset class also depends on your time horizon for holding the investment.

Five

Reduce Your Investment Costs

You should understand this basic fact about funds:
The bite taken out of your investment by fees often
determines whether you have gains or losses.

—Arthur Levitt, chairman, Securities and
Exchange Commission (1993–2001)

A simple way of improving your return on investment is reducing the fees you pay while investing. You should know the cost of every investment you make. Nothing on this earth is free. Not lunch. Not good advice. Certainly not bad advice. And it's fair that you should have to pay for guidance on making investments as long as you're not being *over*charged. You would think that it shouldn't be hard to figure out if you're being overcharged, yet fees are often hidden.

Over time, these fees can take a tremendous bite out of your investments, even out of your retirement funds. I suppose that's why so many of them are hidden. Understanding these costs is essential in choosing a fund or deciding whether to remain in a particular fund. All other things being equal, keep your costs low.

INVESTMENT RULE 4: Reduce Your Costs

Since some costs are notoriously obscure, this chapter describes the different fees charged by the most popular investment vehicle: mutual funds.

> **DEFINITION MUTUAL FUND**: a pool of funds collected from many investors for the purpose of investing in securities such as stocks, bonds, money market instruments and similar assets[xix]

Fees Disclosed in the Prospectus: The Expense Ratio

The first place to look for information about fees is a fund's prospectus, which contains information about an investment's offering. The Securities and Exchange Commission (SEC) requires all mutual funds to publish and make available a prospectus to all potential investors upon request. In the front of the prospectus is a schedule of fees and expenses. (Sales loads and other costs are listed separately.)

Since it's disclosed in the fee schedule, the expense ratio—the cost of operating a mutual fund—is often the only cost investors think they are paying when they buy shares of a mutual fund. The expense ratio is typically used to pay marketing costs,[xv] distribution costs, and management fees. Indeed, it could (and arguably *should*) cover all fund expenses, including fees for managers, analysts, traders, transfer agents, compliance officers, customer service reps, lawyers, technology providers, research resources, and printers, as well as profits for the fund company, brokerage, and possibly the broker or financial planner. Expenses are deducted in relatively miniscule amounts every business day, and the fund's net asset value is adjusted accordingly.

According to a 2014 Morningstar article, the average open-end mutual fund's expense ratio has gradually decreased to 1.25 percent (in 2013) from a peak of 1.47 percent in 2003.[xvi] Sadly, this does *not* represent the total cost of investing in a mutual fund. In truth, it likely only represents one-third of a fund's costs.[xvii] Costs not covered by the expense ratio are generally called *hidden fees*, as they require some detective work to expose.

Hidden Fees

Hidden fees are those charges *not* mentioned in the prospectus, yet they can amount to as much as *double* the expense ratio. So even if the expense ratio is 1.25 percent, you could be paying as much as 3.75 percent in fees and costs! Some fees are undisclosed because of the admitted difficulty in estimating them. Others fees are more controversial and, frankly, I can't offer you a good reason why they are not disclosed. What I can tell you is to be vigilant in keeping an eye out for these common types of hidden fees:

TURNOVER OR TRADING COSTS

Mutual funds are compilations of different investments, for example, stocks, bonds, and cash equivalents. The fund manager, using his best judgment, decides to sell or buy different assets throughout the year. Every transaction, however, incurs transaction fees. Sometimes a fund will trade most or even *all* of its assets in one year. The fund manager does not know in advance how many trades will be made or even how much each trade costs to make. Therefore, instead of estimating the anticipated transaction fees in the prospectus, such fees are listed as a "fund turnover" or "trading percentage."

> **DEFINITION** TURNOVER RATIO: the percentage of the fund's holdings that have been sold and replaced with other holdings during the course of the year

Turnover ratio. A fund with a higher turnover ratio purchases and sells more stocks, bonds, and other financial instruments. The more transactions that a fund engages in, the more fees it incurs. The turnover ratio is indicative of a fund manager's investment philosophy. A fund with a high turnover ratio is more likely to be actively managed by a manager who believes he can beat the market. Because using speculation to manage funds is considered a poor investment philosophy, it's wise to be wary of these funds.

Conversely, a fund with a low turnover rate incurs fewer transaction fees and is more likely to be operated by a fund manager tracking the market. Funds with low turnover rates also offer significant tax savings. That's because every time a fund manager sells a stock or bond, he must report the money earned as a taxable gain. These capital gains can be passed on to the fund's shareholders through higher fees.

THE BID/ASK SPREAD

If you want to sell stock, you don't typically sell directly to a prospective buyer. Instead, you sell it to a brokerage firm, which then finds a buyer to purchase the stock. Because the stockbroker doesn't know whether he will be able to find a buyer willing to pay more for the stock than the broker paid you, he must offset this risk by paying you less than what he is hoping to receive when he resells the stock. The more volatile the stock, the lower the price the broker is willing to pay. This is known as the bid/ask spread.

> **DEFINITION BID/ASK SPREAD: the difference between what the broker paid you for the stock and what he sells the stock for to the next buyer**

It's similar to a markup you'd pay in a store; the store buys something wholesale and then sells it to their customers at a marked-up retail price.

As the volume of stock that the broker purchases increases, the chance that he will be able to find enough buyers to purchase all of that stock at your desired price diminishes. This is because the current price of a stock is usually quoted based on that stock's last transaction. If you need to sell one hundred shares, you only need to wait for one person to be willing to buy one hundred shares at your desired price. However, if you have ten thousand shares, you will either need to wait considerably longer for enough people to be willing to buy ten thousand shares at your desired price, or you will try to sell all ten thousand shares to whoever is willing to purchase shares at a price close to the price you want. The more shares you have to sell, the lower the price you will have to accept, because the number of people willing to purchase shares at each price is limited.

Funds with high turnover ratios sell large blocks of shares more regularly than funds with low turnover ratios. Funds with high turnover ratios lose more money every year to costs associated with the bid/ask spread than funds with low turnover ratios. The end result is that the costs associated with the active effort to achieve outstanding returns end up diluting those returns.[xviii]

Transaction Costs

Transaction costs are not included in the expense ratio nor are they disclosed in most prospectuses. They average approximately 1.44 percent annually.[xix] Although there can be several types of transaction costs, the three most common ones are: brokerage commissions, market impact, and spread cost.

Brokerage commissions. Brokerage commissions come from mutual fund managers who buy and sell stocks for mutual fund investors in a company's brokerage account(s). Calculating the additional expenses attributable to this "turnover" can be difficult. They can be estimated using information found in the Statement of Additional Information, a document that mutual fund companies must make available upon request but don't typically distribute to investors.

Market impact costs. Market impact costs are a consequence of the large amounts of trading conducted by such mutual funds. They save on some costs due to the volume of transactions, but the flip side of that is that their large sales or purchases can immediately affect market prices. As a result, they end up buying higher or selling lower than they had planned. This can be a lose-lose situation for investors because they may get unfair pricing on both the buy and sell side of stock transactions. Ideally, this is offset by savings obtained by volume trading, but the true net effect is often difficult to discern.

Spread costs. Like market impact costs, spread costs occur when a fund buys and sells stocks. It is essentially the opportunity cost as measured by the difference between the best-quoted ask price and the best-quoted bid price.

INVESTMENT ADVISOR FEES

This fee applies only to those working with fee-based investment advisors who select mutual funds for their clients. Advisors typically charge an annual fee between 0.25 percent and 2.5 percent for managing an investor's portfolio. These advisory fees are disclosed in statements provided to the investor. Unless the investor meets certain exceptions (that generally involve placing at least $750,000 worth of assets under management), advisors cannot charge performance-based fees.[xx] Nor are they permitted to waive their fee based on performance (i.e., to create a contingent-fee structure[xxi]). The rationale is that contingent fees would give investment advisors an incentive to speculate or take big risks to achieve the performance necessary to earn a higher fee or avoid losing compensation.

COMMISSIONS, AND THE STATEMENT OF ADDITIONAL INFORMATION

Mutual funds typically do not disclose much information about commissions, yet brokers make a commission on every transaction.[xxii] One significant problem with commissions is the perverse incentive it creates for advisors who only make money based on transactions. Advisors might recommend a transaction even if the more prudent course is to do nothing. Equally problematic is the incentive for advisors to upsell products, thereby generating the higher-paying commissions. Chapter 3 discusses these moral hazards associated with brokers in more detail.

To learn about commissions (and some hidden fees), be certain to request the Statement of Additional Information, which mutual funds are required to provide free of charge upon request. Some disclosures in the Statement of Additional Information information will likely come as a surprise. For example, some mutual funds have "soft dollar arrangements" that enable the fund to pay for research costs through the commissions it pays to its broker. By moving research costs to commissions, the fund manager gets to keep a larger portion of the management fee while making the fund's expenses appear lower.[xxiii]

> **DEFINITION SALES LOAD:** a sales charge or commission that charged to an investor when buying or redeeming shares in a mutual fund

Chapter 6 explains how to distinguish funds according to sales loads. For now, it will suffice to understand that some funds apply a one-time charge at the time you buy into a fund (a "front-end load"), while others charge when you redeem your shares (a "back-end load").

In 2004 the *Wall Street Journal* commissioned a study that found that brokerage commissions "can more than double the cost of owning fund shares."[xxiv] One thing to keep in mind is that fees are not waived or reduced if your account performs poorly. Rather, fees and commissions can compound your losses. If your fees and commissions total 4 percent, you must earn 4 percent just to break even—and that's before accounting for inflation! So, if your money earned a return of 6 percent in 2014, but your fees totaled 4 percent, you'd have a net gain of 2 percent, beating inflation by only 0.4 percent (and underperforming the S&P 500 by 9.5 percent). And that's *before* those gains are taxed.

Little by little, fees and commissions—whether disclosed or hidden—chip away at that bottom line and can even turn what appears to be a profit into a loss. That doesn't mean all mutual funds are bad—it just means you have to be savvy when choosing one. In the next chapter, you'll learn how to distinguish among different types of mutual funds.

Summary

- Understand all the fees you pay for mutual funds: expense ratio, brokerage commission, market impact costs, spread costs, and investment advisor costs.
- Find these fees in the prospectus and the Statement of Additional Information.

Six

DIFFERENT INVESTORS AND
DIFFERENT MUTUAL FUNDS

Mutual funds are constantly offering new shares for sale to the public.[xxv] As table 1 below indicates, there is an astronomical number of different funds from which to choose.

Investment Options[xxxi]	
Total number of stocks	14,089
Total number of mutual funds	30,586
Total number of new funds	54,364
Total number of fund closures	23,778

Data is from the Survivor Bias Free Mutual Fund Database created by the Center for Research in Security Prices (CRSP) as of 12/31/13.

As explained in chapter 5, every fund charges fees to cover expenses, transaction costs, and so on. However, because the manner in which a fund charges fees can affect its price, it is important to be mindful of the different "share classes" of mutual funds. The major difference among them is *when* you pay the fees. Think of them like hotels, where you can be charged upon (or before) check in or when you check out.

A-shares. When you buy A-shares, you pay up front. The upfront fee is usually around 3.5 to 4.5 percent of the amount invested, depending on how much you invest. If you buy $100,000 in A-shares, you'll pay about $4,000 in upfront fees. As in virtually all other areas of commerce, the more money you spend, the greater the likelihood you'll enjoy a discount on the fees. In industry parlance, this means that a broker might offer a reduced "front-end load" of 3.5 percent if you invest $200,000. The fee goes toward the broker and brokerage commissions.

In addition to the front-end load, there are management fees. These average from 1.0 to 1.5 percent of assets managed and are used to pay operating expenses and the fund manager.

Many A-share funds also charge a 12b-1 fee. This covers marketing and distribution costs.

> **DEFINITION** 12b-1 FEE: An annual marketing or distribution fee on a mutual fund, named for the section of the Investment Company Act of 1940[xxxii]

B-shares. With B-shares, there is no front-end fee at the time of deposit. Instead, these funds usually charge higher management fees (typically over 2 percent). They also charge a back-end fee. This means there's free admission, but you have to pay to leave. (This is similar to a frequent complaint about annuities, which charge a surrender fee for withdrawals within a certain period.) The back-end fee is often discounted or eliminated after a certain period of time (the "surrender period") to encourage investors to remain in the fund until that period expires, all the while paying the higher management fee.

To be sure, B-shares are not *necessarily* a worse deal than A-shares. The point is that you have to get into the weeds and really compare them (with tax implications in mind) to know for certain. The main difference is really *when* you'll be paying the fees.

C-shares. C-shares are like B-shares in that there is no upfront fee and they charge similar management fees. That allows more of your money to grow (hopefully) from the start. But C-shares generally charge a lower back-end fee of around 1 percent.

Y-shares or institutional class shares. Some mutual funds are only available for large institutional investors—for example, pension funds—or to high net worth individuals through their investment advisors. Because they do not deal with the public (and the higher turnover rate associated with public or "retail" funds), they typically have lower internal costs. They can, therefore, pass those savings on to the investors in what basically amounts to wholesale pricing.

The Y-share funds generally have a high minimum initial deposit requirement (usually $1 million to $5 million per investor). These funds do not charge front-end or back-end fees, and their expense ratios are typically under 0.75 percent.

It is possible for those with under $1 million to invest to buy an institutional fund through a brokerage firm or registered investment advisor. These firms buy into Y-share funds as part of a managed mutual fund account for which they charge a management fee. Some institutional share funds are available through "discount" brokers, though the brokers require the fund to increase its expenses by around 0.25 percent so the brokerage firm gets paid without charging the investor a transaction fee.

No-load funds. No-load funds don't pay the financial advisor. Instead, the fund charges you—the investor—a fee. That makes them the most transparent of the funds. No need to hunt for commissions and hidden fees since it's spelled out right up front.

The Benefit of Funds with Low Turnover Ratios

A fund with a higher turnover ratio purchases and sells more stocks, bonds, and other financial instruments during a given period than a fund with a lower turnover ratio. More transactions mean more fees. Because using speculation and gambling to manage funds is a poor investment philosophy, it's wise to be wary of these types of funds.

Conversely, a fund with a low turnover rate incurs fewer transaction fees and is more likely to be operated by a fund manager who is tracking the market. Funds with low turnover rates also offer significant tax savings, considering that each time a fund manager sells a stock or bond, he must report the income earned as a taxable gain. These capital gains could be passed on to the fund's shareholders through higher fees being paid from the fund's income.

> **KEY PRINCIPLE: Less turnover often means less taxes on gains to be passed onto investors.**

If your funds are going to be held in a taxable account, you may want to consider tax-managed funds, which engage in strategic trading to minimize taxes.

According to Stephan Horan of the CFA (Certified Financial Analyst) Institute, the trading costs of stock funds amount to 2 to 3 percent of assets each year. These fees include advisory fees, operating expenses, sales costs, and marketing and other fees. These fees have to be paid even when you *lose* money in the fund. If the fees total 3 percent, the fund has to earn 3 percent just for you to break even. And that's before accounting for inflation.

Summary

- It's not how much you make on paper—it's what you get to *keep* and spend that matters.
- Hidden costs and commissions can be virtually impossible to identify yet add significantly to the expenses of a mutual fund.
- To reduce your investment costs:
  1. *Read the prospectus.* If you need help, bring it to a trusted financial advisor and ask him or her to review it with you.
  2. *Get a fee report from a financial advisor.* A properly prepared fee report will compute the amount you are paying in fees each year. This can be a painful exercise, but it's important.
  3. *Consider institutional shares.* Many retail mutual fund shares (A-, B-, or C-shares) can be purchased at a lower price in the form of institutional shares. Confused? Chapter 7 goes into more detail on this option, which can often seriously reduce the amount you're paying in fees.

Seven

DETERMINING YOUR INVESTMENT OBJECTIVES

We all want the greatest expected return for the lowest level of risk, but all of us have different tolerances for risk. The first questions to consider when determining your investment objectives are:

1. *When* do you expect to need the money and for what purpose?
2. What type of risks are you most concerned about—inflation, interest rates, or market risk?

Answering these questions will help you identify your current level of risk tolerance. Based on your anticipated needs, your investment advisor can determine your time horizon and your commensurate risk tolerance.

To accommodate the different levels of risk tolerance, we use four basic risk models: conservative, moderate, growth, and aggressive.

Time Horizons

CONSERVATIVE PORTFOLIO: ONE- TO THREE-YEAR TIME HORIZON
With a time horizon of one to three years, it is typically advisable to put up to 25 percent of your money into stocks. The market may drop within a single year, but it is most likely that the investment will hold its value after two or three years. The remaining 75 percent of your funds should go into a mix of cash equivalents and short-term bonds.

MODERATE PORTFOLIO: THREE- TO FIVE-YEAR TIME HORIZON
If you plan to buy a house in four years, you can probably tolerate the risk, and reap some reward, from putting up to half of your investment into stocks and the remainder into bonds. This mix is intended to grow and preserve your money at a faster rate than short-term investments would. The additional time makes the risk easier to bear. Since bonds often move contrary to stocks, this arrangement helps control volatility within your portfolio. Adding more stocks also helps offset inflation risk.

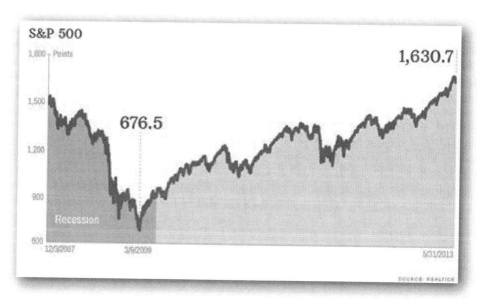

GROWTH PORTFOLIO: SIX- TO NINE-YEAR TIME HORIZON

Six to nine years is a comfortable investment period. Looking back at history, the stock market typically recovers from slumps within this time frame. For example, as the chart above illustrates, the S&P 500 recovered from the 2008–2009 "financial meltdown" in five and one-half years. Even with the Great Depression, the stock market plummeted, but eventually rose again. Plus, the divergent returns of stocks versus bonds help control your portfolio's volatility.

AGGRESSIVE PORTFOLIO: TEN-YEAR OR LONGER TIME HORIZON

Young investors have long time horizons and as such should have aggressive portfolios. This portfolio is 100 percent stock-focused; that is, it is totally focused on growth. That may sound very risky, but it is a good hedge against inflation. (A 100 percent stock portfolio can still be well diversified by varying the asset classes of the stocks.) In addition to minimizing inflation risk, the aggressive portfolio gives you the best chance of higher returns in exchange for higher market risk and volatility.

A 100 percent stock portfolio should have a time horizon of at *least* ten years to weather downturns in the market. In the *worst*-case scenario, $100,000 invested in stocks would still be worth at least $100,000 ten years later. You would not be pleased with this outcome, and nor would I. While it is possible, it is probably the worst-case scenario even though it's the riskiest form of allocation. Remember the investor's dilemma? In these circumstances, the key is to continue to *hold*.

Your Portfolio during Retirement

At the opposite extreme is retirement money. You're not going to spend all of it in ten years, six to nine years, three to five years, or one to three years; it must last the rest of your life. For this investor, the goal is to generate a stable income for the rest of your life. Investing for that goal generally involves a portfolio with 50 to 70 percent stocks and the rest in fixed income. Many of my clients use a 60 percent stocks and 40 percent fixed income mix, which is a very traditional pension mix.

Let's consider what happens with a sixty-forty ratio in which you are taking a 5 percent distribution each year. Distributions come from the bond side of your portfolio, so at this point you are holding eight years of income (5 percent distribution from the 40 percent of your portfolio invested in bonds equals eight years). One reason why we hold so much in bonds during retirement is that it allows us to buy time to weather downturns in the stock portion of our portfolio. You'll want to be able to hold onto your stocks long enough to benefit from the subsequent recovery.

Implementing an Investment Strategy

Throughout this book, I've alluded to different investment options, such as mutual funds or index funds. You have several options, so let's consider them here.

> **DEFINITION** SYSTEMIC RISK VS. SYSTEMATIC RISK:
> Systemic risk generally refers to an event that can trigger a collapse in a certain industry or economy, whereas systematic risk refers to overall market risk.[xxxiii]

1. BUYING INDIVIDUAL STOCKS

You can open a brokerage account and buy your own stocks, but as we know, stocks carry a lot of risks. Relative to options that aggregate many stocks, you are holding a lot of extra nonsystemic risk without an offsetting reason to expect additional returns. Because individual company problems are unpredictable, individual stocks are a poor way of implementing an investment strategy. Moreover, this is a labor-intensive option, and it will require that you judiciously avoid the investor's dilemma.

2. ACTIVELY MANAGED FUNDS

Another approach is buying actively managed funds, but the research says that active management does not work. The simple fact is that the vast majority of active managers underperform their benchmark, even though active funds are more expensive than the more passive options.

3. INDEXING

Indexing is a third way to implement your strategy. Indexes are pegged to a specifically defined set of stocks. They require little management, and therefore the fees are lower relative to other options. But indexes have their own problems. If you choose a sector fund—which is limited to a particular market sector such as technology—or even the S&P 500, you run an unsystematic risk due to insufficient diversification. Remember, from 1966 to 1982, the return on large US stocks after inflation was *zero*. One of the best ways to keep your costs extremely low is simply to cap-weight a portfolio to large companies, because it requires no effort whatsoever.

> **DEFINITION CAP-WEIGHT: A type of market index whose individual components are weighted according to their market capitalization, so that larger components carry a larger percentage weighting.**

Size-Based Indices

If you choose a capitalization-based index, such as the S&P 500, you may be diversified in terms of market sectors, but you are missing out on potential gains from smaller or value companies. (Remember how the monkeys beat the S&P 500?)

Sector Funds

Sector-fund investing refers to using an index pegged to the performance of companies in a particular market sector, such as technology, oil, or mining. This involves betting on market sectors and is one of the riskiest investment strategies, due to the lack of diversification. If you own only a handful of stocks in a sector that is decimated, your investment could be wiped out (think of what happened to horse-drawn-carriage makers after the advent of the automobile).

As economists have shown, it is safer to diversify *across* sectors *and* sizes to ensure you have a healthy mix of investment classes with a low or negative correlation. That way, there will always be some investments that will do well and offset the impact of those that perform poorly.

Reconstitution

Another issue with indexing is reconstitution. The S&P 500 is an index of the five hundred largest US companies. What happens when some of these companies are removed from the index? Everybody who runs an index fund must sell those companies within a short period of time and buy the companies that have edged their way into the top five hundred. Hedge fund managers take advantage of this, buying up potential contenders to the top five hundred before they make the cut and selling the shares at a higher price when there is increased demand from index funds. The index is essentially forced to buy high by its own rules.

4. Institutional Mutual Funds

The fourth way of implementing your strategy is the one we use at Rosen Investment Management: pure asset-class funds, or institutional funds. As we know, mutual funds represent the simplest way to diversify broadly. Many mutual funds hold over ten thousand different stocks. But not all mutual funds are created equal. A brokerage creates identical twin funds; one is marketed to the public (the retail fund), and the other is marketed to institutional investors (rich people or other funds). The goal is to keep the small investor out of institutional funds because small investors tend to panic and pull their money out more frequently (and usually at just the wrong time), which generates a high turnover and transaction costs.

Summary

- Different investment vehicles and levels of risk are appropriate according to when you expect to need the funds.
- Four things to remember for implementing an investment strategy:
  1. Buy individual stocks—this exposes the investor to nonsystemic risk.
  2. Actively managed funds tend not to outperform benchmark and have high transaction costs.
  3. Indexing exposes the investor to unsystematic risk due to lack of diversification.
  4. Institutional mutual funds are broadly diversified and designed for investors who don't make emotional trades.

Eight

THE (SCIENTIFIC) METHOD BEHIND
MODERN INVESTING

To better understand why asset allocation and diversification are so important, we turn to mountains of research by Nobel Prize–winning economists.

Modern Portfolio Theory and Diversification

In 1990, Harry Markowitz, PhD, was awarded the Nobel Prize in economics for his research on the optimization of portfolios along what he calls the "efficient frontier." He knew that people sought the best returns possible given their risk tolerance and showed that diversification could be used to create a portfolio that minimized risk for each given level of return. He also demonstrated that the only way to improve returns was to increase risk, as measured by stock volatility.

To understand the importance of diversification, we must understand the types of risks associated with any investment. The most intuitive risk with a stock or market sector is that the underlying company will experience hardship or failures for reasons unique to it or to its industry. Maybe it is the target of a large government enforcement action. Or perhaps its CFO is caught embezzling money or misreporting earnings. Or perhaps a natural disaster wipes out an essential resource, like a particular crop or a critical piece of a supply chain (e.g., oil pipelines).

A famous example used to describe diversification is the street vendor comparison. Vendor 1, Amy, sells sunglasses and sandals, while vendor 2, Brittany, sells sunglasses and umbrellas. Amy might sell both of her products to the same customers at the same time. Her sales are positively correlated, because they are both in demand on sunny days. Brittany, by contrast, will rarely sell both items to the same customer on the same day. Her sales are negatively correlated.

> **DEFINITION CORRELATION: A connection or relationship between two or more things. Investments that are "positively correlated" will be affected by the same systematic risk, such as a slowdown in manufacturing in Japan. Investments that are "negatively correlated" will not be affected by the same conditions, and their prices won't respond in the same way.**

While Amy may make more money than Brittany over the course of a sunny summer season, one rainy summer could put her out of business. Brittany, by contrast, will not make as much money as Amy on sunny days but has minimized her chances of losing money on any given day.

> **DEFINITION UNSYSTEMATIC RISK: company- or industry-specific hazard that is inherent in each investment[xxxiv]**

UNSYSTEMATIC RISKS

Things like rainy weather are called "unsystematic" risks. They are unsystematic because they don't affect the market as a whole—just an industry or a specific company. A recent example is energy stocks. In 2016, the price of oil plummeted to per-barrel prices not seen since 1999. As a result, energy stocks plummeted in value. Because these unsystematic risks are, by their very nature, unpredictable, it is risky to bet on just one company or one industry. That's why diversification is far more prudent than betting on what you think the next hot stock or sector might be.

KEY PRINCIPLE: The fewer investment vehicles you have, the larger your unsystematic risk.

A single bank is more likely to go bankrupt than its entire cohort of similarly sized banks. There is also more volatility in investing in a single stock as opposed to the whole market. If you spread your risk across hundreds of stocks, the companies that underperform will have little effect on your portfolio. On average, you do not reap any extra reward for that extra volatility. That's what we call "uncompensated risk."

KEY PRINCIPLE: Don't take risks if there's little prospect of a proportionate reward.

UNCOMPENSATED RISK

Why expose yourself to unnecessary risk if there is no upside? Without diversifying, you subject yourself to volatility and unsystematic risk typically with no good reason for doing so. Without a crystal ball, there's no legitimate reason to think that certain stocks are going to outperform the market as a whole.

SYSTEMATIC RISKS

Systematic risks are those specific to one company or market sector. If you hold only one stock, you run the risk that something will happen to the company you invested in and not to its counterpart. If McDonald's has a food recall, Burger King does not suffer. You can reduce systematic risk by diversifying your portfolio.

THE UPSIDE OF RISK

Now that we have established the importance of minimizing systematic and unsystematic risk, let's discuss the upside associated with risk—larger payouts over time. First, it bears repeating that *you will typically make more money from stocks than bonds.* There is equity risk in owning stocks, but over long periods of time (e.g., twenty years or more), you can expect a higher return.

Second, *small companies are riskier than large companies, but the pay-offs associated with the successful ones are much higher* than the returns from large companies. Similarly, companies with less liquid capital (so-called value investments) tend to yield larger returns than financially strong companies.

By choosing assets that are unrelated or negatively correlated, you can protect your overall portfolio from the risk of being harmed by un-predictable events.

> *KEY PRINCIPLE: When diversifying a portfolio, invest in assets with negatively correlated price movements so that when one goes down, the other has the potential to offset it by increasing.*

Markowitz showed that it's possible to have two assets that look volatile individually, but when combined in a single portfolio, reduce volatility and increase the potential rate of return.

In investment terms, if you have a large US stock portfolio all in the S&P 500, your portfolio will be vulnerable to risks affecting the US economy. But it's possible to reduce your level of risk without reducing your potential returns if you diversify further. You could accomplish this by selling off some shares of US funds and purchasing small international stocks. Large US stocks and small international stocks are not highly correlated, so when combined, they reduce risk in your portfolio.

> *KEY PRINCIPLE: By blending many individual investments into a portfolio, you create an overall portfolio that is less risky than its individual elements and can even yield greater returns.*

The simplest way to enjoy these benefits is by buying into low-cost, well-diversified mutual funds.

The Three-Factor Model

Eugene Fama and Kenneth French expanded on the research into diversification, identifying three key factors that affect a portfolio's returns. You can think of each of these factors as a type of investment risk: market factor, size factor, and value factor.

Market factor: The market factor tells us it is inherently riskier to invest in the stock market than in fixed-income instruments, such as US Treasuries (bills, notes, and bonds). Stock purchases demand a higher return because more risk is involved. If stocks did not offer a higher return than Treasuries, everyone would invest in the much safer T-Bills. But stocks have the potential to provide a higher rate of return than fixed income instruments. So the market risk factor informs your decision as to how to divide your portfolio between stocks and bonds.

> **DEFINITION FIXED INCOME:** Fixed income investments (typically municipal bonds or treasuries) that pay a predictable premium on a regular schedule

Size factor: The size factor takes into consideration the size of the companies in which you're investing. Small companies generally have the potential for higher returns than do large companies but are riskier investments.[xxvi] Larger companies are less likely to experience tumultuous business changes, making them appear more stable. In addition, they're typically more capable of weathering adverse economic conditions and unexpected events. Because of their lower level of risk, the market demands less return on investments in large companies.

Value factor: The value factor refers to the extra risk exposure, and the extra risk premium, of investing in high book-to-market or "value" stocks.[xxvii] High book-to-market stocks refer to companies with a lower market price than other companies of similar size.[xxviii] These types of companies are usually ones that are experiencing lower earnings and some kind of financial distress. As a result, they're riskier and offer investors the potential for a higher return.

Research suggests that it is sensible to shift money into companies just when they are having a hard time. That may seem counterintuitive, especially when comparing a value company to one that has better growth and better returns.

KEY PRINCIPLE: There is risk and reward inherent in distressed companies. Investors are less willing to buy into the stock, given the level of risk involved, so the price drops. This builds the degree of risk into the price, as per the efficient-market hypothesis.

In contrast, a company that is doing well has already been rewarded with a higher stock price (also as per the efficient-market hypothesis). So if there's a marked improvement in the distressed company, the upside will be much higher, relative to a proportional improvement in the healthy company. That's why people on reality shows buy run-down houses, fix them up, and then flip them at a significant profit.

A hypothetical example: To emphasize the importance of diversification and asset allocation over long periods, imagine that you had one dollar to invest in 1926 that you would cash in in 2015.

- If you had invested it in large-growth stocks, that dollar would have increased to $3,530 in 2015.
- If you had put it into large-value stocks, it would have grown to $12,910.
- Investing in small-growth stocks would have yielded $14,580.
- In small-value stocks, that dollar would have grown to a whopping $139,000.

There's a big difference in returns depending on how you invested that dollar.

Pulling It All Together: Asset Allocation and Diversification

It's virtually impossible to predict which asset class will do well over a specific period. Sometimes different asset classes move together; sometimes they don't. Some tend to move in the opposite direction from others. For instance, when the dollar weakens, international stocks tend to do better.

There have been long periods where certain categories of stocks experienced extraordinarily high returns. In the late '70s and early '80s, small international stocks really shined, boasting 70 to 80 percent returns each year. Then in the late '80s, when Japan was booming, large international stocks did extraordinarily well. Next, in the early '90s, small US stocks did very well. In the late '90s, it was large US blue chip stocks.

> **DEFINITION BLUE CHIP**: Nationally recognized, financially sound companies. They are stable, and their growth tends to mirror that of the S&P 500.[xxxix]

Then the tech bubble burst in 2000. Then in the mid-2000s, the US dollar dropped in value, and international stocks (including emerging markets) did well. More recently, the housing bubble burst in 2008, and the market nose-dived but began making a comeback in 2009.

KEY PRINCIPLE: Diversify portfolio by investing in different financial instruments, and differently sized and valued companies.

Many investors use asset allocation as a way to diversify their investments among asset categories.

ASSET ALLOCATION

Asset allocation refers to the composition of your investment portfolio. You can divide your investment in many ways, including stocks, bonds, cash, and cash equivalents. An asset-allocation-based strategy aims to balance risks and rewards by adjusting your portfolio's makeup based on your risk tolerance and time frame—two things that vary depending on your personal investment objectives.

Some people decide not to diversity for reasons that depend on their investment goals and time horizon. A twenty-year-old who starts investing for retirement may choose to invest solely in stocks. By contrast, a family saving for a down payment on a new home might want to have that money in cash equivalents, which are short term and highly liquid. These two asset allocation strategies do not spread risk across different asset classes and, hence, are not diversified.

KEY PRINCIPLE: A well-diversified portfolio spreads your investment among different types of investments, and within different asset classes.

If you are well diversified, you don't have to try to predict what type of asset class will do well, or when it will increase in value. In other words, you don't have to time the market. Different asset classes move independently, so gains and losses in one asset class can offset gains and losses in another. That mitigates losses when the stock market turns bearish. Having a cornucopia of different assets reduces your portfolio's *overall* level of risk without costing you anything extra.

Making Asset Allocation Work for You

Once you decide on your asset mix (the subject of the chapter 9), you *must* rebalance it periodically to keep your portfolio working for you. Rebalancing means bringing your portfolio back to your desired asset allocation mix. It is important to rebalance, because some investments will grow faster than others, which will cause the ratios of different asset classes within your portfolio to be out of alignment with your investment goals. By rebalancing, you keep your portfolio within your risk-reward comfort zone.

KEY PRINCIPLE: Periodically rebalancing your portfolio brings it back into alignment with your investment goals.

For example, let's say you determined that stock investments should represent 60 percent of your portfolio. After a market rally, stocks grow to represent 80 percent of your portfolio.

There are three ways to bring your portfolio back into alignment with your chosen asset allocation strategy:

1. Sell off investments from overweighted asset categories, and use the proceeds to purchase investments in underweighted asset categories.
2. Add capital to make new investments in underweighted asset categories.
3. If you make continuous contributions to your portfolio, alter your contributions so that more investment goes to underweighted asset classes until your portfolio is back in balance.

In the example above, where stocks have rallied, it can be psychologically difficult to force yourself to rebalance your portfolio. It's hard to rationalize shifting money from an asset that is performing well into one that isn't. But don't think of it as giving up on well-performing assets; think of it as locking in some of your gains. Cutting back on the current "winners" and adding more of the so-called losers *forces* you to buy low and sell high.

INVESTMENT RULE 5: Buy Low and Sell High

WHEN TO REBALANCE

You can rebalance your portfolio based either according to the calendar or based on your investment ratios. Many financial experts recommend that investors rebalance their portfolios on a regular basis—every six or twelve months. The advantage of this method is that the calendar reminds you when to rebalance.

Others recommend rebalancing when the relative share of an asset class increases or decreases more than a certain percentage that you set in advance. The advantage of this method is that your investments determine when to rebalance. In either case, rebalancing works best when done on a regular, but relatively infrequent, basis to minimize transaction costs.

You can direct your investment advisor to rebalance your portfolio accordingly to either of these methods. At Rosen Investment Management, we automatically rebalance our investors' portfolios every quarter after considering the tax implications of selling off assets, unless the asset ratio has not changed very much.

For example, if your investment strategy is 50 percent fixed income and 50 percent stocks, and at the end of the quarter the proportion is 48 percent fixed income and 52 percent stocks (because the stock value grew faster than the bond value), it probably doesn't make sense to rebalance. But if, in the following quarter, stocks rally, and your portfolio mix is now 39 percent fixed income and 61 percent stocks, we would rebalance to a fifty-fifty ratio by buying more fixed-income securities.

Putting These Models to Work: Finding the Right Mix for You

The three-factor model shows us that by systematically exposing a portfolio to the three risk factors—market factor, size factor, and value factor—it is possible to increase expected returns without increasing risk.

We believe that an investment portfolio should be built on a sound foundation of research, a strategic and closely adhered to financial plan, and rational expectations. Speculation or hunches, and the perpetual buying and selling of stocks, are costly and inefficient. There is no single "right" answer for how much risk is appropriate for a portfolio; each investor has his or her own unique circumstances dictating the level of risk to assume.

Summary

- Understand the difference between systematic risk and unsystematic risk.
- Invest in assets with negatively correlated price movements.
- Periodically rebalance your portfolio to bring it back into alignment with your investment objectives.
- Diversify your portfolio with different types of investments and across asset classes.
- Also diversify according to market factor, size factor, and value factor.

Nine

HOW WE EVALUATE *YOUR* PORTFOLIO

Mutual funds hold thousands of different stocks and have many hidden costs (expense ratios, turnover, load fees, etc.) that can significantly reduce your returns. There are countless ways to allocate your assets and diversify a portfolio. Additionally, we have seen that portfolios must be rebalanced to maintain the proper asset mix. So how do you know if your current portfolio is right for you? How do you know how close or far you are from where you need or want to be? The answer is that you must take a comprehensive assessment of your portfolio and compare it to the relevant benchmarks as well as other potential options.

The Portfolio MRI

Rosen Investment Management uses a proprietary diagnostic tool called a portfolio MRI to analyze your investments and assess their volatility, total fees, turnover, and diversification. This personalized investment analysis will help you better understand your investments as well as the costs and risks associated with them. We begin with understanding your personal goals and needs. Armed with this information, we can then analyze how different mixes or styles of investment portfolios may have performed in the past. That enables us to calculate the expected return for your portfolio and gives us an idea of how well your portfolio meets the goal of providing broad diversification that delivers market returns with reduced risk.

Volatility

The portfolio MRI will measure the historic volatility of your portfolio and give you an idea of the historic volatility and performance of different asset classes. That allows us to estimate the risks you are taking relative to the returns you've seen and compare your portfolio's performance to the performance of other benchmarks over similar time periods. Not only can we assess how well the volatility we see matches up with your risk tolerance, but we can also determine whether alternatives asset mixes would be likely, based on historical data, to reduce volatility or yield higher returns (or both!).

Total Fees and Turnover

As we've already discussed, expenses can eat away at your portfolio. In fact, total fund expense (including but not limited to turnover ratio) is the most important variable to consider when comparing funds because it's the one that actually makes a difference.

> **KEY PRINCIPLE: Total fund expense is the most important variable to consider when comparing funds.**

The portfolio MRI will uncover what you are paying in *total* fees—not just the fees you know about. If you don't know what your fees are, there is no logical way to find less expensive ones. So we simply drill down into your portfolio to reveal all of the fees that affect your returns.

Since turnover within a portfolio can significantly affect returns due to transaction costs, we will also learn what percentage of your portfolio is turning over in a year.[xxix] We can then assess that turnover in comparison with an index, like the S&P 500, as well as one or more institutional mutual funds. Once we know your actual costs, we can advise you how to lower those costs to keep more of your money working for you.

> **KEY PRINCIPLE: *The easiest way to increase your return is to reduce your fees.***

DIVERSIFICATION AND PORTFOLIO OVERLAP

Diversifying is easier said than done. It's easy to own stocks across different market sectors such as a tech company, oil company, clothing company, and a food company. But there are more layers to diversification. You should diversify in terms of size and geography in addition to market sector.

If you own mutual fund shares, assessing your diversification can involve some work, because the true scope of your investments is hidden. By drilling down into the funds you are invested in, we will learn how many funds hold the same stocks. We call this portfolio overlap. That redundancy can reduce your true diversification and add complexity to managing your investments.

> **KEY PRINCIPLE: Asset allocation and diversification are the most important factors in a portfolio's long-term performance.[xxx]**

Most people know that diversification is important and believe that their portfolio is diversified. In reality, most people fall far short of achieving true portfolio diversification. Even people invested in one or more mutual funds often hold fewer than four thousand unique stock or bonds in their portfolios, yet wrongly believe they are well diversified. In the modern financial world, many mutual funds hold over ten thousand different stocks. (The one I currently favor holds over twelve thousand.) More importantly, while a wide spread of stocks is important, the total number of unique holdings alone doesn't actually tell you anything about how *diverse* those assets are. They could all be in foreign banks or fast food companies for all we know.

We will break down your asset allocations in detail, and make sure the mix meets your investment objectives. Then, using indices for different investment categories, we will compare the performance of your portfolio's asset mix to the historical performance of other mixes. That way we can make sure you are truly and properly diversified.

Opportunity Costs

By comparing the performance of your investments to appropriate benchmarks, we can see if you've made as much money as you could have made. One simple reason that people are not seeing the returns they ought to see is that they are invested in retail funds rather than comparable institutional funds. If you are in a retail fund, it is likely you are missing out on some of the gains that can be realized with institutional funds, which would reduce your costs. That alone would increase your expected return without changing your risk.

Putting the Portfolio MRI in Context

The portfolio MRI is part report card and part recipe book. It breaks down information about your investments and stacks them up against inflation-adjusted historical data reflecting different asset mixes, funds, indices, and so on. I like to walk through the portfolio MRI with my clients step by step. I want everyone to understand the logic behind the investment choices they are making and how their portfolio fares in terms of the five rules of investing. By looking at your portfolio over time, we can see how closely it adheres to the fundamental rules of investing. Let's review them:

Summary

1. DON'T TRY TO TIME THE MARKET

Often, in examining a portfolio's performance over time, it becomes clear that a fund manager is trying to time the market. For example, if your fund was invested in large-value stocks in 2010, but by 2012 it had shifted to large-growth stocks, the fund would be experiencing "style drift." The manager is trying to time the market and predict whether it will go up or down. He is speculating and gambling with your money.

Alternatively, we often see the amount of cash holdings fluctuating. This can be a sign that the fund manager is jumping in and out of stocks. Alternatively, it can mean there is a large outflow of investors in the fund. Either way, keeping 10 percent (a relatively large amount of your portfolio) in cash reduces your protection against inflation.

2. BUY AND HOLD

You may be adhering to this principle, but the same might not be true for your fund manager. To assess how much buying and selling has been going on within a mutual fund, you must review the turnover percentage. A fund turnover of 50 percent means that 50 percent of the stocks in your portfolio have changed since last year. Every time your fund manager buys and sells a stock, there is a cost. It's called the bid/ask spread. These costs are passed on to you and hurt your returns.

This also means that your fund manager is gambling with your portfolio, buying and selling stocks he thinks are winners and losers. If fund turnover is too high, you've broken another rule of investing without even realizing it.

3. DIVERSIFY BROADLY

If you own mutual fund shares, we will use the MRI to see what they contain. Let's say you own both Fidelity's Contrafund® and Fidelity's Growth Fund, each of which invests in Apple in different proportions. The Contrafund® might have 3 percent of its holdings in Apple stock and the Growth Fund might only have 1 percent. If Apple does well, the Contrafund® has a competitive advantage over the Growth Fund. It will receive a five-star rating, and its fund manager will be called a genius. But it was really by chance that one fund did better than the others did. We see this all the time, and what it means is that not all strategies—or even all funds—are truly designed to diversify your risk. In fact, it's likely that they are designed in part to diversify Fidelity's chances of having a highly rated fund. If Fidelity were really confident in Apple, all of their funds would own the exact same amount of Apple stock.

4. REDUCE YOUR COSTS

It is important to know how much you are paying in fees for your investments. You should know how your investment advisor is compensated and whether he is fulfilling a fiduciary duty to you or is working for the mutual fund or brokerage.

You also need to be aware of all hidden fees that are not readily disclosed in a prospectus. These fees can be found in the Statement of Additional Information that is available to all investors, at no cost, upon request.

5. BUY LOW AND SELL HIGH

This one is simple—if you are doing this, you will be losing money over time. Even if you are not in the red, failure to obey this rule will be revealed by poor performance in comparison with the appropriate benchmarks.

Ten

A lot of the decisions you have to make in this process are emotional. They should be, because they will affect the people you care about the most. That's why no matter how smart and rational you are, it helps to work with someone else. Even financial advisors work with financial advisors. It's economics, but it's also psychology. We are often blind to our own biases and mistakes. The advisor serves as a check and a balance to your own inclinations, protecting you from yourself.

So if you've decided to seek the help of an objective financial advisor, the next question is who. Since many of the best ones can be paradoxically hard to identify, I describe herein some ways to find them. But first, let's discuss *why* some are better than others.

"First, do no harm" is the famous maxim from the doctor's Hippocratic oath. A good advisor is like a good doctor; they first examine the situation and make a diagnosis. Only after that do they prescribe a solution. Imagine you went to a doctor who, without even examining you or asking you anything, handed you a prescription, saying, "Everyone has the flu right now." Before you can explain that you're there for, say, an injury or a rash, he's gone. Would you go back to that doctor? Would you even pay that doctor? Of course not. This has happened to me in many contexts—as a lawyer, a business owner, a homeowner, a patient, and so on.

Sometimes, this problem is compounded with *jargon*. Big, unhelpful words are thrown at you without explanation, often by the same person ushering you out the door. Every industry has its jargon, such as "legalese." Terms of art have specific meanings under particular circumstances, but you are entitled to understand your options. Part of any professional's job is ensuring that his clients (or patients) *understand* the advice or options being presented to them.

How to Know What to Ask

What should you be looking for to avoid these problems? Your first meeting with an advisor should involve lots of questions—about your life, your family, and your goals, so your advisor can have a full picture of what's important to you.

CONFLICTS OF INTEREST

An advisor is not a salesperson. Obviously, a Ford dealer is not going to tell you that a Jeep would be best for you and your family; you know walking in there that he or she will try to sell you a Ford. They call themselves automobile salespeople, not advisors, and we don't expect them to give us purely unbiased advice.

But in the financial realm, it's peculiarly permissible and common for the lines between salesperson and objective advisor to blur. That's because virtually everyone in the industry uses the "advisor" moniker. That gives the imprimatur of objectivity, so you'd think they have your best interests at heart. Some do. Yet many so-called advisors are really stockbrokers who make money from sales commissions and try to cloak themselves in the image of objectivity. They have every incentive to put their and their firm's interests above your own, which unfortunately they often do.

The main difference between a stockbroker (who holds a Series 7 license) and an SEC-registered investment advisor (who holds a Series 65 license) is that only the latter is bound by a fiduciary duty. That means that the latter are required by law to put their clients' interests before their own. (Pension fund managers are also required by law to act as a fiduciary with respect to the participants in the pension plans they manage.)

> **DEFINITION FIDUCIARY DUTY: a legal requirement to act in the best interests of another party.**

A Series 7 stockbroker, on the other hand, is held to a "suitability" standard, meaning that he can sell you investment products that are "suitable" for you even while knowing there's a better option for you.[xxxi] A Series 7 broker might sell you an expensive mutual fund (that generates a higher commission for him) even if there's a less expensive one that's equally suitable. By contrast, a Series 65 investment advisor representative would have to inform you of the other option and even try to make sure you get the best price available at the time he enters the trade.

According to a 2015 survey by Financial Engines Inc., an independent investment advice firm, almost nine out of ten retirement investors said it's very important (69 percent) or somewhat important (18 percent) to work with a financial advisor who is legally required to take on fiduciary responsibility.[xxxii]

How can you tell the difference? First, you should empower yourself with information. Just as you should have some inkling of the type of car you want and your price range when you sit down with a dealership salesperson, you should walk in to an investment advisor's office having already checked the advisor's credentials. Yet according to the Financial

Industry Regulatory Authority (FINRA), only 15 percent of people do a simple background check. Fortunately, there is a simple way to do this. The BrokerCheck website (BrokerCheck.FINRA.org) provides information about the advisor's employment, registrations, and licenses, as well as any investment-related investigations, disciplinary actions, arbitrations, criminal records, or bankruptcies.[xxxiii] Start there, and then make an appointment to speak with someone.

Once you sit down to talk with a potential advisor, you want to look for transparency about potential conflicts of interest and their fees and compensation.[xxxiv] You must insist at the outset that you talk about conflicts of interest. A real advisor will be transparent and forthcoming about potential conflicts. In the financial realm, it is difficult to *completely* eliminate conflicts of interest, but an honest advisor will readily disclose the scope of his or her own potential conflicts.

An excellent way to identify conflicts of interest is to examine how the advisor is compensated. Here are some simple questions you should ask:

1. How do you get paid?
2. How much do I pay you?
3. Are you a fiduciary?
4. Are you entitled to any compensation, based on our working together, from anyone other than me?
5. Do you receive any extra compensation based on the products you recommend to me or that I purchase?

Note that you should ask *each* of these questions; they're not exactly the same. (OK, the last two are basically the same, but it couldn't hurt to ask twice just to be sure.) For example, compensation for many advisors comes partly in the form of sales-based bonuses or commissions for selling you certain products. After hearing the advisor's answers to these questions, you'll have a good idea whether there are likely conflicts of interest as well as how much you will have to pay the advisor and how often (e.g., quarterly or monthly).

Keep in mind that some people are unscrupulous, and some are outright liars. (Even Bernard Madoff was a SEC-registered investment advisor.) But going through these steps helps you minimize the risk of hiring the wrong one. (One way to protect against fraud is to have an outside auditor review your portfolio periodically.) Also note that some people are both stockbroker and investment advisor. They can wear two hats, which means you have to be clear on whether the fiduciary standard applies to your account.

A Good Advisor Can Help You Avoid Big Mistakes

You're hiring an advisor to help you make good decisions and avoid making bad decisions. To do that, they must give dispassionate, objective advice that's tailored to your unique situation. Ask yourself if you can trust the person to get to know you well enough to help you behave financially for the next ten, twenty, or thirty years. That means understanding not just your finances but also your objectives, your values, and your family situation. It's important that you feel comfortable with them because there will be times when they will have to convince you to not do something (like sell when times are looking bad). If they can't do that, why should you pay them at all? Seek out someone whose advice you will actually respect. I've said it before, and I'll say it again: successful investing is about behavior, not skill.

Nobel Prize–winning behavioral economist Daniel Kahneman has suggested that we are all born with certain inherent biases. This wiring makes it difficult to consistently make good financial decisions. So, when the market gets ugly, most people sell. When it rallies, most people buy. This results in exactly the behavior you want to avoid: sell low, buy high. Not good. Your financial plan and your advisor are guardrails that keep you from joining that money-hemorrhaging crowd. You can still move within the lines, but they keep you from stepping out of bounds.

Coordinate Your Financial and Estate Planning

I began providing financial advisory services because I saw problems resulting from a lack of coordination between financial planning and estate planning. Poor financial planning leaves people struggling through their retirement years and even causes estate problems after death. I've heard too many sad stories to allow my clients to end up in distress during their twilight years.

> **KEY PRINCIPLE: *For the most effective results, coordinate your investment planning with your estate planning.***

The estate plan protects your most important assets from taxes, court fees, nursing homes, and so on. But if your investment portfolio is dysfunctional, there may not be many assets left to protect. Too many people pay excessive fees and take on too much risk.

It makes no sense to separate retirement planning from estate planning. The elements that are essential to crafting a solid estate plan are the same ones that are crucial to a financial plan: evaluating your objectives, wishes, and family concerns. At Rosen Investment Management, we take a holistic approach, analyzing all the important details of your situation and integrating asset protection, financial planning, retirement income and distribution planning, long-term healthcare planning, and estate planning.

Summary

- Make sure your financial advisor has a fiduciary responsibility to you and doesn't have a conflict of interest to due to his compensation.
- Coordinate financial and estate planning to protect your assets from taxes, court costs, and nursing homes.

Eleven

Frequently Asked Questions (FAQ) about Investing

1. How do you build a better portfolio using an academic approach?

The single most important thing we learned from the work of academics is that diversification works. To build a more resilient portfolio using the academic approach, deploy your capital over global boundaries because we know that the US, European, UK, and Japanese markets don't move together. Also, deploy your capital between fixed income and equity, small stocks and large stocks, and value and growth companies. We don't know which stocks will go up or down at any specific time in the future, so owning them all reduces your risk of devastating losses.

2. How do you help the average investor allocate as little as $10,000 in a portfolio?

Some of our smallest clients have portfolios that are as diverse as those of a Fortune 500 pension plan with billions of dollars. We recommend starting out by building a portfolio with the following:

- twelve thousand holdings
- nineteen different asset classes
- forty-five countries represented

3. Is it a problem if I'm eating into my principal by making withdrawals from my portfolio?

It's normal for portfolios to occasionally undergo circumstances in which it's necessary to dip into principal. When a portfolio is designed to outpace inflation, it's going to periodically decline in value. Having some investments in bonds or fixed income investments gives you room for spendable income when markets are down. Diversification is key to ensuring that a portfolio can withstand occasional dipping into principal.

4. Can index funds be purchased with this approach to investing?

This approach can be used to invest in index funds, although it's uncommon. Note there are a few drawbacks to using this approach on index funds. First, index funds are typically not diversified well with small international or small international value stocks, or emerging-market categories. Second, index funds may not represent the asset classes you want. And finally, index funds can incur additional costs because stocks change regularly within the index.

5. If I were to invest in gold, how do I use it? What role does gold play in this investment approach?

Because it's a commodity, gold's value rises and falls based upon supply and demand. We don't recommend investing in commodities, because our approach is founded upon the idea that someone should be paying you for the use of your money. That is, when you put your money in the bank, you are paid in interest. When you invest in a company, you have the rights to a share of its profits. That isn't the case with gold, and it's usually much harder to sell than to buy.

6. Should I seek to get out of the market when the economy is starting to look bad?

The market, like everything, has its ups and downs. It moves in cycles. If you want to get out when it takes a downturn, it's typically an emotional reaction. The news and financial analysts have a way of creating fear and panic in investors, which drives the kind of emotional decision making that leads to long-term portfolio erosion. Before making any changes, consult with your financial coach, who can help you make sure you're making logical, informed decisions about your money.

7. Is it a good time to buy stocks when the market takes a big drop?

The short answer is yes because generally speaking, after a big drop stocks will go through great growth periods. But this isn't always true, and it's hard to know when the drop has hit bottom or when the growth will occur. Making sure you have a diverse portfolio will help to ensure stability while the outcome reveals itself.

8. Is it a good idea to have an annuity to protect my principal?

Keep in mind that investing should be about getting a reward for allowing a company to use your money. Without some risk, the reward is low. The problem with annuities is that while they are a "safe" place to keep your money, their returns are usually restricted by tactics such as high fees and caps on returns. On top of that, as an annuity investor you don't get to partake of dividends from the annuity's underlying companies, making the annuity more lucrative for its manager than the investor.

9. I trust the investment firm I'm with because they've been around for a long time. Is my confidence in their qualifications justified?

If you do an Internet search that includes the name of your investment firm and the words "settlement," "misconduct," or "lawsuit," you'll see that they've likely been accused of mishandling money at some point. Even if they are acting scrupulously, many times money is being managed by unsupervised people who have entered the industry with minimal education and experience. It's crucial that you don't have blind faith when it comes to your portfolio and that you have a solid understanding of investment tactics and options so you can be sure your money is being managed properly, whether it's by a globally recognized firm or a local entity.

10. *This has never happened before.* What do I do?

The market will always be affected by dramatic world events; it's nothing new. Looking back over the twentieth century, we can see many wars, man-made catastrophes, and natural disasters that left investors and entire populations feeling insecure and unsure of what to do next. In times like these, it's important to turn to your preestablished rules for investing so that you aren't making emotional decisions. One thing that's certain is that things have always recovered, no matter how bad they seemed at the moment.

11. I'm new to investing and the amount of information I have to take in is intimidating. How can I get started?

Before you get started, review everything you've learned from this book. Being able to see the difference between myths and truths, especially in advertising, will help you avoid investments that are too good to be true. Second, we recommend working with a fee-only advisor, which will prevent you from paying more than the amount necessary for his services. Continue to educate yourself because it's entirely up to you to make informed decisions about whom you will trust to advise you as you work to build wealth.

12. What is a financial coach?

A financial coach guides clients through a disciplined investment process. No matter how well the portfolio is put together, there may be periods of time when the market outlook is negative and fear could cause you to want to get out. A coach helps support you through the process of keeping a disciplined approach that's based on knowledge. Peace of mind isn't created from the portfolio, but through education and financial coaching.

13. What makes financial planning different from financial coaching?

Financial planning is often used as a marketing tool to sell financial products. An individual investor working with a financial planner generally has little way of knowing whether the recommendations made are in their best interest or in the best interest of the planner. They also have little way of knowing whether the financial products could have been obtained elsewhere at lower cost. The majority of planners work for brokerage firms or a broker/dealer, and don't really work for the client. The brokerage firm also typically controls which products can be recommended. Finally, the traditional planning process does little to educate investors and help them deal with the emotional reactions that are at the root of many poor investment decisions.

14. What are your workshops and educational events?

All of our clients are welcome and encouraged to attend educational workshops in addition to one-on-one wealth coaching. All of these workshops are offered free of charge to existing asset management clients. To find out about dates for upcoming workshops, call our office.

Our workshops and seminars cover a wide range of topics, including:

DISCOVERING YOUR TRUE PURPOSE FOR MONEY

Understanding your "true purpose for money" is the crucial first step that paves the way for long-lasting satisfaction when it comes to your financial decisions. The answers to some key questions will help you identify the values that will act as your compass for financial decisions. You'll identify those things that are more important than money itself. Find out how you've been trapped in the investor's dilemma and reveal your own true purpose for money.

CHOOSING YOUR INVESTMENT PHILOSOPHY

A solid investment philosophy provides a stable foundation upon which to base future decisions. Once you have an investment philosophy that fits with your values and is easy to understand, it will simplify every decision you will ever make about investing. This is one of the most important aspects of investing.

David E. Rosen, Esq.

Defeating Your Money Demons
Locked within each of us are deeply rooted belief systems about money and what it means to us. When you bring your money demons to the level of awareness, you can defeat them and create new beliefs that lead to different actions and outcomes.

Understanding the Dimensions of Risk and Return
The terms "risk" and "return" have different meanings to different people. It's easy to get confused. Understanding the dimensions of risk and return clarifies these frequently talked about, yet rarely understood, concepts of investing.

Focusing on Your Future View
Deliberately reveal what is most important so you can clearly focus on reaching your goals. You will shed new light on what it is you want your money to accomplish. In this way, you redefine your idea of investment success.

Examining Your Expectations
Understanding the relationship between expectations and results is crucial to your peace of mind. When it comes to investing or any area of life, your expectations are the deciding factor in how you feel about the outcome.

Creating Your Core Covenants
This program walks you step by step through the process of writing core covenants and teaches you how to use them with the important people in your life.

CUSTOMIZING YOUR LIFELONG GAME PLAN

The final component walks you and your financial coach through a clear process so you can integrate the personal information you revealed into your investment strategy. Your lifelong game plan is a comprehensive, cohesive document that merges both the coaching and financial components of your investing future.

CONSCIOUS INVESTING FOR PEACE OF MIND

This necessary component is a fun introduction to all of the concepts in the workshops and offers the opportunity to better understand what we call "the human side of investing." Take the conscious-investor quiz, learn the conscious-investor formula, and begin to ask the "right" questions about investing.

Part II

HOLDING ON TO YOUR MONEY
FOR LIFE (AND BEYOND)

Twelve

DEATH, DISABILITY, AND TAXES: UNDERSTANDING THE VITAL IMPORTANCE OF ESTATE PLANNING

People generally don't give much thought to their own deaths while they are alive. But when it comes down to the inevitable, not planning properly for estate management and distribution can place a tremendous strain on a grieving family due to money lost to avoidable taxes, excessive legal fees, demands on their time, and stress.

When planning for old age, disability, and death, most people have four goals:

1. If they become disabled, they want to avoid losing the assets they've spent a lifetime building to a few years of healthcare costs.
2. When they die, they want to be sure of exactly who will receive which assets from their estate.
3. They want things to be easy for their family; in other words, they want to pass on their property easily, quickly, and without high legal fees.
4. They don't want to pay any more taxes than necessary (e.g., they want to avoid or minimize state and federal death taxes).

The absence of a solid estate plan puts each of these goals in jeopardy. By creating an estate-planning portfolio, you can rest assured that if you become disabled and when you die, your estate will be handled to your precise specifications.

Throughout the coming pages, you'll become acquainted with everything you need to know to make sound legal decisions about your—and your family's—financial security. Specifically, you'll learn the following:

- your four primary options for long-term planning
- the five *least* desirable outcomes of poor planning
- how to protect your assets if you become incapacitated and/or must enter a nursing home
- how an estate-planning portfolio can protect your estate from heavy expenses

> **KEY PRINCIPLE: *An estate plan protects your estate from heavy expenses and other undesired outcomes.***

Some of the laws I review in this section pertain no matter where you live, but some are specific to the state where I practice, Massachusetts. Be sure to find out what state laws apply to your own estate.

Before we get into these topics, there are a few basics you'll need to understand.

Understanding Your Estate

WHAT IS CONSIDERED PART OF YOUR ESTATE?

Your estate includes every asset you own or in which you hold an interest, including real property, investments, business interests, insurance proceeds, personal property, and possessions. If you jointly own an asset with another party, your share is considered part of your estate. For example, married couples often hold title to property as "separate property" or under "joint tenancy." Understanding the difference before one person dies or becomes ill is essential for keeping your family protected when circumstances change.

- As separate property: one spouse owns the entire property, which was usually acquired before marriage or was inherited by that spouse during the course of the marriage.
- Under joint tenancy: ownership is shared, and when one owner dies, the other owner(s) automatically acquires that person's interest in the property.

What Is an Estate Plan?

Your estate plan is a legally binding plan that defines how your wealth will be managed if you need to be cared for in sickness, plus how your wealth will be distributed after your death. The estate plan also serves to preserve the values that matter most to you, so that after your incapacitation or death, your estate lives on in a manner that you, not the courts, decide.

Know Your Options

When planning your estate, there are four possible basic courses of action:

1. Do nothing.
2. Establish joint tenancy for your assets.
3. Draft and execute a will.
4. Establish a revocable living trust.

Option 1: Do Nothing

Studies indicated that up to 70 percent of Americans don't take any action to prepare for illness or death, either because it's not something they want to think about or because they don't know what to do. Of the remaining 30 percent, most have only executed a simple will or rely on the laws of joint tenancy to pass on their assets to their spouse. However, without a revocable living trust, which I will explain shortly, most estate distributions will be determined by state law, not by the wishes of the deceased.

When the government steps in to determine your wealth distribution, your family's best interests are of little concern. The estate is simply distributed according to the letter of the law. The chances increase that your estate will accumulate high death taxes, legal fees, and probate costs. Plus, the stress resulting from a poor plan can be divisive, and has even destroyed families.

Option 2: Establish Joint Tenancy for Your Assets

As it's formally called, joint tenancy with right of survivorship is a situation in which two or more people share title to an asset. When one of the owners passes away, his or her share of the ownership passes to the other "joint tenant" automatically. "Right of survivorship" means that whoever lives longer gains ownership of the asset.

You might think that a will would override joint tenancy laws. Not so. Since the transfer of a jointly held asset essentially occurs automatically upon death, it's out of the estate before the will is even triggered.

Imagine two cousins own a piece of property as joint tenants. When one dies, his will states that his wife should inherit all of his assets. But because the property is owned in joint tenancy, the surviving cousin (joint tenant) owns the entire property; the surviving spouse has no claim on the property! This and other problems of joint tenancy can be avoided with a good estate plan.

> **DEFINITION JOINT TENANCY**: ownership of property by two of more people. Protects property from probate as deceased's portion of ownership passes to other joint tenant(s).

Option 3: Draft a Will

Movies dramatize a last will and testament as the final say on how an estate will be distributed. In reality, a will isn't as ironclad as many people think and doesn't hold sway over joint tenancy laws or insurance proceeds. In fact, once the will enters into the probate court system, it's not in the hands of your family anymore. It's in the hands of the court and probate attorneys, where it's subject to their discretion and open for public scrutiny. There is no guarantee that your wishes will be fulfilled.

> **KEY PRINCIPLE: A last will and testament does not have the final say on how your assets will be distributed after death.**

The mere drafting of a will, alone, creates even more problems because a will doesn't gain relevancy until after you die. Therefore, it doesn't help with planning for illness or long-term care. In general, the last will and testament is an inefficient and poor planning tool.

Option 4: Establish a Revocable Living Trust

A revocable living trust is the most reliable and thorough foundation for an estate-planning portfolio and provides the most complete financial protection for you and your family.

> **KEY PRINCIPLE: A living trust avoids probate, can finance your final healthcare expenses, and supports the values that are important to you.**

When we set up a living trust in your name, title to all of your major assets is transferred from your name to the name of the trust. You are listed as the trustee and beneficiary, so you still have total control to make decisions regarding your assets (property, investments, cash, etc.). After your death, your successor trustee will take over the trust. Your family won't have to endure the lengthy and costly process of probate court. Because the values that are important to you are written into the trust, you can be assured that your estate will be handled in accordance with your wishes whether you are sick and unable to manage it, or pass away. Your trust can even determine how your healthcare will be financed in the event that you or your spouse becomes disabled, thereby minimizing the expense to your estate.

The Outcomes of Poor Planning

There are five major problems that can arise as a result of no, or poor, estate planning. Here's what you want your family to avoid:

1. **Living probate.** If you become disabled, the probate court will decide how your estate is to be managed so your medical and nursing-home-care bills can be paid. This can include the decision to sell your home, for example, to pay nursing care expenses. The living probate process is, in and of itself, costly, lengthy, and stressful for your heirs.
2. **Death probate.** As mentioned earlier, the court process used to distribute your estate after your death is lengthy and expensive for your family.

> **DEFINITION** PROBATE: a legal process that pays debts owed by your estate and applicable Death Taxes, and distributes the remainder of your estate to your designated beneficiaries.

3. **Death taxes**. In Massachusetts, the combined state and federal death taxes can consume over 50 percent of your estate's worth.

4. **Nursing-care expenses**. If you or your spouse needs to be in a nursing home or rehabilitation facility, or need home care, expenses mount quickly and can deplete your estate.

5. **Death of your values**. Without proper planning, the values and principles you hoped would be reflected in the distribution of your assets may be glossed over or worse, ignored altogether.

Avoiding Living Probate

Probate court isn't just for processing wills after death. If you become mentally disabled and can no longer make decisions about your own care (and how to pay for it), the court will appoint an agent to take over your personal affairs. That includes making decisions about your assets. This kind of living probate is also known as conservatorship or guardianship proceedings. The living probate process is very time consuming and expensive, plus your assets and debts are exposed to the general public through the process.

JOINT TENANCY AND LIVING PROBATE

If one of the joint tenants in a joint tenancy ownership is mentally incapacitated or otherwise unable to make a major decision regarding property (such as the sale of property), nothing can be done without the help of the probate court. The court actually takes over the incapacitated joint tenant's role and will manage the property until the incapacitated owner recovers or dies. The risk of leaving your property in the hands of the court, which does not necessarily have your best interests or those of your cotenant in mind, should be avoided at all costs.

A WILL AND LIVING PROBATE

Since a will only goes into effect after your death, it plays no part in a living probate. It also does nothing to protect your assets during difficult times, which can be very expensive if you or your spouse needs nursing or home care.

KEY PRINCIPLE: The best way to avoid probate is to have a living trust that holds title to your assets.

A Living Trust and Living Probate
A living trust, if well written, can help you avoid the expense and lengthy process of living probate. There is a section in the living trust that lays out exactly how you want your estate and healthcare to be handled in the that event you're unable to manage your assets yourself. Your fellow trustees are bound by law to follow your instructions, so the probate court doesn't have to assume a role in your life. This relieves your family of the stress of working with the courts plus leaves you with the assurance that things will be handled according to your wishes.

Disadvantages of Death Probate
Death probate is the court process of distributing and managing an estate after your death. Even if you have a written will, it must go through the probate process. Debts need to be paid, and assets need to be distributed to your designees. The court takes care of these tasks for you. Simple as it sounds, death probate is a tedious and lengthy process that can tie up assets for months and consume the value of your estate in court and attorney fees.

There are five basic steps that every estate goes through in death probate:

1. **File the petition.**
   Before the probate process can begin, someone must formally file a written petition to the probate court and pay the filing fee. If you have no living trust, the court will then approve or

appoint someone from your family to be your personal representative, more formally known as your will's executor or administrator. Because the probate court's paperwork and filing procedures can be so complex, most personal representatives find it necessary to hire an attorney even in cases where it is not legally required.

2. **Publish notice to creditors.**

   This step of the probate process can take months to complete. First, every debt you owe must be documented. The court then notifies the deceased's creditors by mail and by placing an ad in the local newspapers. This gives creditors an opportunity to file a claim for payment with the court. The probate court decides how long this portion of the proceedings will be left open for creditors to file claims. In most states, this period lasts several months. Death is not an escape from financial obligations.

3. **Appraise and inventory all assets.**

   While the notice to creditors is being published, every asset in an estate must be listed and appraised. During this phase, assets are usually frozen, meaning they can't be sold or distributed to heirs without written permission from the court. This includes everything from real estate and investments to furniture, antiques, jewelry, and more. Formal written appraisals can be costly and the estate must pay them out of pocket.

4. **Distribute payments on debts, claims, and taxes.**

   After the court has approved creditors' claims, it gives approval for the estate to pay the claims. On top of creditors' claims, death taxes must also be paid, if applicable. The estate proceedings must stay open until all liabilities are paid. But sometimes wills are contested, which means that anyone (usually heirs who feel slighted by the will) can file a lawsuit with the probate court to try and gain access to what's left of the assets. These contests not only prolong proceedings for months or years but have also been known to tear families apart.

5. **Do the final distribution and close the estate.**

Once any contesting lawsuits are settled, the court officially orders the estate's executor to pay all remaining debts, claims, taxes, attorney's fees, personal-representative compensation, and other expenses. If the estate doesn't have enough liquidity to pay these expenses, the court will order that the estate be subject to a public auction or estate sale to raise the cash. If this is done in a depressed economic climate, the estate's assets may bring in less than they might have under more favorable circumstances. Whatever is left after all debts are paid will finally be distributed to beneficiaries (if there is a will) or to whom the court designates as heirs (if there is no will). Then the probate court can finally close the case.

The High Cost of Death Probate Fees

According to a recent national survey, the average cost of death probate is typically between 5 and 10 percent of an estate's *gross* value. Of that amount, around 60 percent goes to pay attorneys' legal fees, while the rest goes to pay personal representatives and other costs.

Every state has a different method for calculating probate court fees, including the fees that attorneys and personal representatives demand. In some states, there are no limits to what a probate attorney can charge a client. In others, fees are limited to a maximum percentage of the estate's worth. In any case, the fees can be a tremendous burden on your family. For example, a married couple could potentially pay probate fees upon the death of each spouse, each time chipping away even further at their intended heirs' inheritances.

Not only are these fees extremely high, but in states where the fee calculation is percentage-based, they are especially unfair because fees are calculated based on your estate's *gross*—not net—value. For example, if you own a property that's worth $1 million on the market, but you owe $600,000 on it, your probate fees will be calculated using a percentage of the $1 million figure, not the $400,000 in equity owned by the estate after debts, liens, or other expenses are paid. Because of this lopsided calculation, your estate will be forced to pay higher fees.

Probate Is a Long Process

Probate can be a very long and arduous process for your family. It usually takes at least eighteen months to complete; in some cases, probate proceedings go on for years. Even under the best circumstances, it's almost impossible to fully process an estate through probate court in under twelve months due to the complexity of the process and stringent court requirements.

Your Estate in Probate Becomes Public Record

Whatever pains you took during your lifetime to maintain your privacy will be irrelevant if your estate winds up in death probate. All records of probate proceedings and every detail of your estate are open to public scrutiny. Anyone who is interested can see your probate file, which includes details of every asset you owned at death, the name of every creditor you had (plus the amount you owe), and exactly what each of your heirs is intended to inherit.

KEY PRINCIPLE: In probate, your estate becomes a matter of public record.

Unscrupulous salespeople often use this information to sell goods and services to grieving family members who have inherited money or other assets. If you owned a business, even confidential business information can be revealed during the probate process, making your surviving business vulnerable to competitors after your death.

Multistate Probate

Adding to the already time-consuming and expensive process of death probate, if you own property in more than one state, a new probate must be filed for each state in which you owned property. Because each state has jurisdiction over property within its borders, this "ancillary probate" requires that the same death probate process be followed and a local attorney be retained to settle the estate.

More Disadvantages of Death Probate

Death probate has several other serious disadvantages:

- Your family loses control of your estate and cannot sell assets or use estate cash to purchase assets without the court's permission.
- Opportunities to buy, sell, or transfer assets may be lost to the slow-moving court proceedings.
- Many families suffer emotionally during the probate process because the court proceedings are a constant reminder of their loss.
- Because of the stressful process, fighting within families is a common side effect of probate, especially if one person has been named the executor of the will, which leaves other family members feeling powerless.

Joint Tenancy and Death Probate

There are cases in which joint tenancy can help you avoid death probate. For example, if one person in a married couple dies, anything they owned in joint tenancy passes automatically to the surviving spouse. But when that surviving spouse dies (or if they both die at the same time), the entire estate is required to go through the full probate process.

Joint tenancy has even more disadvantages in other circumstances. In a case in which parents and their children own assets together, joint tenancy does not protect them from probate, can result in unintended beneficiaries, and can create legal complications around gift and death taxes. Overall, joint tenancy is an extremely poor estate-planning tool.

The Will and the Death Probate

This part is simple: if you have only a last will and testament, your estate is guaranteed to go into probate, period.

A Living Trust and Death Probate

A living trust is an excellent way to avoid the probate process, whether you're still alive or have passed away. In a living trust you'll transfer the title for all of your assets out of your name and into the name of the trust. This is done by changing the name on the deeds to your real property and by signing transfer of ownership documentation for other assets.

This leaves you, personally, with little ownership of anything. But once everything is in the name of the trust, you and/or your spouse can be named as trustees, which means you have the power to make all decisions about every asset the trust owns. You can even revoke the trust at any point and reclaim formal ownership. If you become ill or die, your previously named successor trustee(s) will take over the management of the trust's assets but will control them to your specifications.

One significant advantage of having a living trust is that upon your death, there's no need to go through the probate process. Your family will avoid unnecessary probate court and attorneys' fees, and there's no need to delay the distribution of your assets; intended heirs can receive their inheritances instantly. Your successor trustee must follow your written instructions on how you intended your estate's assets to be distributed.

Estimated[xxxvi] Death Probate Fees in Massachusetts			
GROSS ESTATE	PROBATE FEE	GROSS ESTATE	PROBATE FEE
$ 100,000	$ 7,835	$ 800,000	$ 43,000
$ 200,000	$ 13,835	$ 900,000	$ 47,500
$ 300,000	$ 20,000	$ 1,000,000	$ 52,000
$ 400,000	$ 24,500	$ 1,500,000	$ 77,000
$ 500,000	$ 29,500	$ 2,000,000	$ 102,000
$ 600,000	$ 34,000	$ 2,500,000	$ 127,000
$ 700,000	$ 38,500	$ 3,000,000	$ 152,000

The Facts about Death Taxes

FEDERAL AND STATE DEATH TAXES—AND EXEMPTIONS

After your death, your family may be liable for federal estate tax and state inheritance tax. These taxes are in addition to any expenses you may have to pay, such as probate and legal fees. Also, under current federal law, they can be between 41 and 55 percent of every dollar of your estate over the exemption thresholds outlined below. Estate taxes are often referred to as death taxes.

THE FEDERAL DEATH (ESTATE) TAX

After your death, the federal government allows your beneficiaries to receive up to $5,340,000 (indexed for inflation) without paying death taxes. Every dollar above that will be taxed unless there is a plan in place before your death to avoid high death taxes.

MASSACHUSETTS DEATH (ESTATE) TAX

Many estates that do not owe federal estate tax will, nevertheless, owe Massachusetts estate tax. This is because the amount that passes as tax-free for Massachusetts's purposes is much less than what passes as tax-free under federal law. While the federal estate tax exemption is currently $5,340,000 per person, the Massachusetts exemption is only $1 million. Although the $5-million estate of a Massachusetts resident will pay no federal tax, that same estate nevertheless will owe substantial Massachusetts tax on over $4 million in assets.

The Massachusetts estate tax applies to all estates of Massachusetts residents. The $1 million exemption is a filing threshold. That is, a Massachusetts estate tax return must be filed—even if no tax is actually due—for any Massachusetts decedent whose gross estate (the gross value of all property owned at death or the ownership of which otherwise legally is attributed to the decedent) exceeds $1 million.[xxxv]

ESTATE TAX AND MARRIAGE

When one spouse passes, no estate tax is required to be paid to either the federal government or the Commonwealth of Massachusetts. This exception is called the unlimited marital deduction because no matter the size of the estate, a surviving spouse will not have to pay death taxes upon the death of his or her spouse.[xxxvi] This is important in the short run, but in the long run, death taxes will catch up to the family. When the last living spouse dies and the estate passes to his or her beneficiaries, federal and state taxes may be due, depending on the size of the estate, perhaps at an even higher rate if the estate has increased in value.

Planning for a Small Estate

Even if you have a small estate that would be exempt from Massachusetts death taxes (if the estate is worth less than $1 million), you may still be forced to go through living probate or death probate (or both). Proper estate planning cannot only save you on potential estate taxes, it can also help your family avoid the heavy time demands and financial burdens of probate court.

Summary

WHY IT'S IMPORTANT TO SET UP A LIVING TRUST

1. Eliminate living probate.

A living trust helps your family avoid court expenses and time-consuming procedures if you become mentally or physically incapable of managing your assets. The successor trustee you have chosen in advance will manage all of your affairs to your written specifications.

2. Protect assets if you are disabled.

Getting quality nursing home and rehabilitative care if you or your spouse become disabled or incapacitated can be extremely expensive. A living trust can help you qualify for government assistance with those expenses. In this scenario, neither caretakers nor the government can deplete your estate, and Medicaid may even pay for your nursing home or in-home care.

3. Avoid death probate.

Without a living trust, your estate will have to go through the very long and expensive process of death probate in court, even if you have a last will and testament. When you have a living trust, you avoid those costs, and your estate can be distributed quickly by a trust administrator without court interference or public scrutiny.

4. Maintain privacy.

Neighbors, relatives who feel slighted, and ambitious sales people and scam artists can view every detail of your estate when it enters probate court (including your assets, debts, beneficiaries, and more). This lack of confidentiality is completely avoided by a living trust because it is administered privately.

FACT! Beware of scam artists who try to exploit publically available information about your estate.

5. Avoid estate taxes.

The federal government allows your beneficiaries to receive up to $5,340,000 (indexed for inflation) without paying death taxes. In Massachusetts, if you die with $1 million or less, your family will usually be exempt from death tax (although there are exceptions). But with a properly planned living trust, a married couple can leave double those amounts to their heirs without paying death taxes.

6. Control your estate—even in death.

With a living trust, long-term distributions can be made to your exact specifications, even after your death. For example, you can turn assets over to your children when they reach a particular age you designate so you can still support their education and future wellbeing. You can also set up your insurance proceeds to be paid directly to the trust to control how those proceeds are distributed.

7. Protect your children from their creditors and ex-spouses.

You may want to ensure your children from prior relationships are treated fairly after your death. Your living trust can be written specifically so that distributions intended for your children (including children from a prior relationship) will be protected from their former spouses or current creditors.

8. Ensure that your wishes are carried out after your death.

If your living trust contains a no-contest clause, disinherited heirs and beneficiaries and their lawyers cannot get more than you intended for them to have from your estate.

9. Find true peace of mind.

When you know that your estate is safe and will be managed by someone whom you know and trust, you and your family can enjoy your later years without worrying how your estate will be distributed after your death. A living trust is the best measure for securing peace of mind.

Thirteen

TAXES

If you live or work in the United States, you are subject to taxation by the federal government and at least one state government (many local governments also levy an income tax). Here's the bright side of paying income taxes: you must have made some money if you owe taxes. Now, on to the rest of it.

Throughout life, including during retirement, tax obligations depend upon individual circumstances. Tax laws can be complicated, and they often change significantly from one year to the next. (That's why it's important to consult a tax attorney or CPA when developing a comprehensive retirement plan.) For now, it should suffice to say that there are two general categories of taxes relevant here: taxes you pay during your life (income tax) and taxes that are owed after death (estate taxes).

Taxes You Pay during Life: Income Taxes

Income taxes are calculated based on your taxable income, which (broadly defined) is your total income minus deductions permitted by the applicable tax code. Individuals may deduct an exemption called a personal allowance and may also deduct certain expenses (e.g., interest on a home mortgage, state taxes, charitable contributions, etc.). (Some expenses are deductible only to a limit.)

Capital gains (money you've made from profitable investments) are taxable, and capital losses (money you've lost on poor investments) are deductible but only to a point. Short-term capital gains (profits from assets held for one year or less) are taxed at the same rate as income (10 to 39.6 percent in 2015). Long-term capital gains (profits from assets held for longer than one year) and income from corporate dividends are taxed at a lower rate (generally 15 percent or 20 percent, though upper-income investors may pay additional surcharges) than income.

You self-assess your income tax. (Although this system is widely criticized as inefficient, it's unlikely to change anytime soon.) The amount you calculate may, of course, be adjusted by the tax authorities if they disagree with you.

FACT! Social Security income is taxable as income.

One thing that seems counterintuitive but bears noting is that Social Security income *is* taxable as income. Many people incorrectly assume they will pay lower taxes upon retirement, but depending on how you've saved for retirement and whether you have a pension, you may very well remain in the same tax bracket when you retire that you were in during your working years.

How Taxes Continue to Hurt in Retirement

A retired couple with a taxable income of $5,000 per month ends up, after federal taxes, with net income of about $4,119. (Massachusetts imposes an additional 5.15 percent state income tax, leaving only about $3,865 in actual, spendable money.) Once our retired couple pays for routine expenses, such as groceries, utility and phone bills, property taxes, car payments, gasoline, and healthcare costs, that $3,865 is *gone*. (For this reason, taxing Social Security income can seem especially maddening.)

FACT! The top 25 percent of wage earners pay about two-thirds of the nation's taxes.

If you've had the good fortune, foresight, and diligence to earn a pension, Uncle Sam gets a piece of that too, just as he gets a piece of your dividend payments, interest, and Social Security payments. On top of that, your individual retirement accounts (IRAs) and 401ks may contain taxable assets. Naturally, inheritances are also taxable.

Reducing Your Tax Burden in Retirement

When planning for retirement, you must factor in taxes. Many economists expect that savers will be penalized in the coming years, because excessive government borrowing and spending (e.g., for military operations, Medicare, and Medicaid) will lead to giant debts (currently over $18 *trillion* federally, or more than $150,000 per taxpayer) that will be passed down from one generation to the next.[xxxvii]

Do not assume you'll be paying less in taxes when you retire. (Even if you start off paying less, keep in mind that it is possible to migrate into a higher bracket as you withdraw untaxed portions of your retirement portfolio.) Smart planning for retirement, which should be done with a trusted accountant or tax attorney, will help minimize your tax burden.

Taxes You Owe after Death: Estate Taxes

The IRS levies a tax—at a rate of 40 percent or more—on the right to transfer property upon death. You, or, more accurately, the administrator of your estate, must detail everything you owned or had a financial interest in at the time of your death. This includes, but is not limited to, cash, securities, real estate, insurance policies, trusts, annuities, business interests, and intellectual property. The fair market value (which is not necessarily the same price you paid) of these things must also be appraised and disclosed. Taken together, these things form your "gross estate."

Once your gross estate is ascertained, some deductions (and possibly reductions in value) apply. Examples of such deductions are debts (including mortgages), estate administration expenses, and property that passes to a spouse or qualified charity. What remains after such deductions is the taxable estate. The value of all lifetime taxable gifts (gifts given after 1976), if any, is then added to it, and the tax is calculated.[xxxviii]

Simple estates containing cash, publicly traded securities, and easily valued property (but not jointly held property), can be handled without filing an estate tax return. If the estate has combined gross assets and prior taxable gifts totaling $5 million or more, then an estate tax return is required. As explained in the following section, Massachusetts's threshold for the estate tax requirement is much lower: $1 million.

The Massachusetts Estate Tax

Fortunately, the Massachusetts estate tax is not as high as the federal tax. It starts at 8 percent for assets over $40,000 and peaks at 16 percent for assets over $10 million. If the taxable estate is valued at less than $1 million,[xxxix] the tax doesn't apply, but once that threshold is crossed, the tax applies and begins chipping away at the estate beginning at the $40,000 mark.

One quirk of this type of tax assessment is that some people with estates over the threshold may prefer to divest some of those assets during their lifetimes to avoid the tax on their estates. For example, an estate with taxable assets of $1.2 million would owe approximately $50,000 in taxes. Faced with that reality, some people would choose to divest the estate of $200,001 by making qualifying gifts, for example, to bring the taxable estate under the $1 million threshold.

Reducing Your Estimated Estate Taxes in Massachusetts	
TAXABLE ESTATE	**ESTATE TAX (ESTIMATED)**
$ 1,000,000	$ 35,000
$ 1,500,000	$ 70,000
$ 2,000,000	$ 100,000

Massachusetts Estate Tax Burden

If you are a Massachusetts resident (or couple) with virtually no chance of having an estate worth over $1 million, you can skip ahead to the next section. But if there's any chance that your estate will be valued at over $1 million, then you should keep reading to learn how to reduce the estate tax burden.

There are three general alternatives to paying the tax:

1. SPEND YOUR MONEY, AND GIVE GIFTS.

Gifts of up to $14,000 per year are not taxed. Through advanced planning, you can make piecemeal annual transfers of assets to save your loved ones some tax expenses in the long run. For example, assume that

Michelle owns a home worth $500,000, and has $250,000 in savings and investments, plus another $250,000 in assets in an IRA. Taking money from her savings investments could be detrimental for Michelle's financial security. She could, however, transfer an interest in her home to her children in $14,000 annual increments.

FACT! IRA withdrawals are taxable income.

Unfortunately, that strategy would not be advisable if the house had significantly appreciated since Michelle bought it, due to the lifetime-gift-and-capital-gains tax consequences. Under that circumstance, Michelle could accelerate her IRA withdrawals instead. If there is anything left in the IRA upon her death, those funds will be passed on to Michelle's children and taxed based on their respective individual tax rates. If Michelle successfully reduced her estate to under $1 million with this adjustment, around $35,000 in estate taxes would be avoided entirely. (To be fair, we would expect the accelerated distributions to result in some lost earnings in the IRA, but on balance, the result should be a significant savings.) This way, Michelle gets the benefit of spending more of her money during her lifetime while still saving responsibly and ensuring that her heirs are not taxed unnecessarily.

2. GIVE AWAY MORE MONEY AND BIGGER GIFTS!

The $14,000 gift exclusion mentioned above just means that you don't even have to report gifts on your tax return unless you give away more than $14,000 in a year. But the federal lifetime gift tax only kicks in after you give away over $5.34 *million* worth of gifts. You should be very proud indeed if you find yourself required to pay the federal gift tax. (In fact, even if you give away no more than $15,000 per year every year, you would have to reach age 356 for this to be a federal tax issue.) So there are situations in which giving away larger gifts reduces your total estate tax by bringing your taxable estate into a lower tax bracket.

Unfortunately, this approach will not help you avoid the estate tax altogether. That's because although there is no state gift tax in Massachusetts, lifetime gifts count toward the value of your estate. In the above example, we saw how Michelle could gradually reduce her estate's value by making smaller gifts over time. If she instead gave one lump-sum gift on her deathbed, the amount would be dragged back into her estate and it would remain above the threshold. That's why this deathbed-gifting approach is no substitute for good, advanced planning.

3. CREATE A TRUST FOR THE SURVIVING SPOUSE (COUPLES ONLY).

Money passing from a deceased spouse to the surviving spouse is not taxed. But if that money remained in the surviving spouse's estate upon his death, it would then be taxed. If the surviving spouse does not need the money, the couple can plan to avoid this by passing enough assets to others (e.g., their children) so that the surviving spouse's estate remains below $1 million. This strategy works only up to a point; if you give away over $1 million, the estate will owe a tax anyway.

Alternatively, the surviving spouse may refuse or disclaim some of the money. In that situation, the money, like any other property, would typically pass to the children. This approach may require difficult calculations at a difficult time, which is one reason why most clients opt for the third option—structuring the estate to have assets pass directly into a trust established for the surviving spouse's benefit. Such a trust would provide income for the surviving spouse during life without the remainder being taxed upon death. Again, this requires advanced planning with trusted counsel.

Fourteen

ASSET PROTECTION DURING
DISABILITY AND ELDER CARE

In the years leading up to retirement (and maybe even during retirement), you work hard to build a nest egg. Many factors determine whether your retirement savings are sufficient, such as whether you have a pension, the rate of inflation and the buying power of your money, investment returns, your life-span, and your healthcare needs.

People are living longer than ever. The life expectancy for a man born in 1955 is seventy-eight. Women, on average, live five years longer than men. And there's a 50 percent chance that a person born in 1955 will live to age eighty-five. In fact, people age eighty-five and older are the fastest growing demographic in America. For a couple reaching age sixty-five, there's a one in two chance that one spouse will reach age ninety-four, and a one in four chance that one will reach age ninety-seven. Actuaries call this longevity risk. I call it good news! But you need to plan for it, because longevity can be expensive.

> **DEFINITION LONGEVITY RICK: the risk that you will outlive your assets**

In cases in which people have become mentally or physically disabled due to illness, injury, or old age, the cost of care can destroy the wealth they spent a lifetime building. According to the Council for Disability Awareness, one in three people will become disabled at some point in his or her life. Given that alarming statistic, planning for nursing care is a crucial step in protecting your wealth.

The government will only pay up to a certain point for nursing care; after that, it's your responsibility, whether you choose to go into a nursing home or prefer to receive care in the comfort of your own home. By planning, you can arrange in advance for whatever outcome you most prefer.

FACT! When planning for the future, people tend to underestimate their life expectancy by an average of five years.[xl]

That means planning for the possibility that you will reach age ninety or higher and need long-term care for some years. (A good rule of thumb for couples is to plan your assets to last you until you are one hundred.) Naturally, there are situations in which health or family history suggest a shorter life span, in which case your planning should account for that.

Hope for the Best; Plan for the Worst.

This chapter will help you understand how to prepare for the tragedies of life. Healthcare crises, in my view, are the most pressing concern. But such events can also include the loss of a job, divorce, theft, or even problems resulting from poor investments. There are tools that can help mitigate the financial impact of these situations, protecting you and your loved ones from the expensive prospects of long-term care, divorce, and creditors. Tools include long-term-care insurance, homestead declarations, durable powers of attorney and healthcare proxies, family protection trusts, and irrevocable trusts.

Important Long-Term-Care Planning Documents

DURABLE POWERS OF ATTORNEY AND HEALTHCARE PROXIES

Health and safety are paramount concerns, so step one in the planning process is choosing your designated agents and executing durable powers of attorney and healthcare proxies. If something happens that renders you unable to manage your affairs, you are considered incapacitated. Sometimes, as in the case of a coma, it isn't clear whether incapacity will be temporary or permanent.

An effective and reliable way to protect yourself and your assets is to appoint someone to act as your agent in the event of your incapacitation, and execute a durable power of attorney (POA).

> **DEFINITION HEALTHCARE PROXY designates the power to make medical decisions in your behalf to someone you designate**

Another tool is a healthcare proxy. Each of these delegates the power to make important decisions to people you trust and designate. A durable power of attorney can include the power to make financial, legal, and even healthcare decisions in your behalf. A healthcare proxy is limited to making healthcare decisions. Your signature on these legal documents is presumed genuine if acknowledged before a notary or another person authorized to take acknowledgements.

Of course, signing a power of attorney or healthcare proxy does not take away your right to make decisions for yourself. So long as you have the capacity to do so, you can revoke these documents, or execute new ones as you see fit. The point is not to divest yourself of any authority or responsibility but to make sure your wishes and affairs are carried out, if something happens to you, by someone you trust.

When someone is incapacitated and they have not executed a power of attorney or healthcare proxy, their family members may have to go to court and seek the appointment of a guardian to make financial, legal, or healthcare decisions. That can be expensive and stressful, especially if there is disagreement within the family. It can also interfere with taking necessary steps to protect assets since many actions under guardianship will need court approval.

Under the federal Health Insurance Portability and Accountability Act of 1996 (HIPAA), medical professionals cannot release healthcare information to anyone without a signed release or a court order. For this reason, HIPAA releases, also known as "medical authorizations," are included in durable powers of attorney and healthcare proxies. In practice, what this means is that most healthcare providers will accept HIPAA releases signed by your proxy if they attach a copy of the POA or healthcare proxy.

If, however, you want to give different people different degrees of authority—for example, give your child access to records but leave healthcare decisions only to your spouse—you may want to execute separate healthcare proxies. This can be helpful if you simply want family members to be able to communicate with medical providers—for example, with respect to an upcoming medical procedure. These situations arise quite often, so your estate plan should include a HIPAA release as well as a durable power of attorney and healthcare proxy.

JOINT ACCOUNTS

You may have a joint account at a bank or another financial institution. Each joint account holder can make withdrawals. If one joint owner dies, the account simply belongs to the surviving joint owner(s). This can be very handy and efficient, but it is not, by itself, a suitable alternative to powers of attorney, trusts, or wills.

One downside is that the money in a joint account is subject to claims by the creditors of each joint account owner. In the event of a lawsuit, bankruptcy, or divorce, each joint account holder can be liable. (One good rule of thumb is to end the joint account status of children by the time they get married. In the event of a divorce, that can prevent the ex-spouse from touching the money in the formerly joint account.)

Another problem often arises when a parent with multiple children establishes joint accounts with each. If money is drawn down from one account to pay, for example, long-term healthcare costs, an unequal distribution upon the owner's death may result. The joint owner of the depleted account may feel slighted in comparison with their siblings whose accounts remained flush.

Joint accounts work best where there is only one child to inherit assets. The other suitable situation is one in which the senior owner and her children share ownership of a checking account so each child can help pay bills and can access funds to pay funeral and estate expenses.

HOMESTEAD DECLARATION

One of the best asset-protection tools available to a homeowner is the homestead declaration. Quite simply, if you reside in a home you own in Massachusetts, you can file a homestead declaration in the office of the county clerk in the county in which your home is located. That can protect up to $500,000 in equity from creditors. Disabled co-owners aged sixty-two or older may each file a homestead declaration, which can be helpful if the total home equity exceeds $500,000.

The homestead declaration protects home equity from lawsuits and bankruptcy. (Unfortunately, but understandably, lenders usually require that a homestead declaration be removed as a precondition to obtaining a mortgage or refinancing.) It bears noting that the homestead declaration does not apply after the homeowner's death, so it does not protect the estate from creditors. Nor will it protect the proceeds of the sale of a home from creditors.

Nonetheless, it is easy and inexpensive to execute and file a homestead declaration, and every Massachusetts homeowner should do so.

Trusts

As mentioned in chapter 12, trusts can help manage your assets and avoid probate. Trusts are a special way of turning assets into a gift. Through a trust, you can even give a gift to yourself, as explained in the living trust section below. A trust is managed by one or more trustees who manage the trust property for one or more beneficiaries.

Every trust is created by a properly executed document (usually simply called the trust, or trust document, or sometimes the trust agreement). The other requirements are a settlor, a trustee, and a beneficiary. The settlor (also known as the grantor) is the gift giver—the person(s) putting assets into the trust. The beneficiary is the person for whose benefit the trust exists. The grantor and the trustee can be the same person if you are making the gift to yourself. The trustee manages the trust to preserve the assets and make sure they are used to benefit the beneficiary according to the settlor's wishes as specified in the trust.

The Revocable, or Living, Trust

The creator of a revocable trust typically also serves as a trustee and as the principal beneficiary during his or her lifetime. This is often called a living trust. It provides for successor trustees in the event of incapacity and successor beneficiaries upon their death.

The appointment of a successor trustee can be an excellent way to provide for property management. Revocable trusts can be more narrowly tailored than durable powers of attorney, so the settlor can be specific about the use of the trust property. Finally, as emphasized in chapter 12, revocable trusts avoid probate.

FAMILY PROTECTION TRUSTS

Parents can protect the inheritance they leave their children and grandchildren by leaving them in trust rather than outright to their children. These so-called "spendthrift" trusts are designed to protect children from themselves—in other words, from poor spending decisions. The downside is that the child cannot control distributions, so establishing clear terms and choosing a good trustee is essential.

PLANNING FOR LONG-TERM CARE

Many events can trigger the need for long-term care. Some children are born with an ailment that requires long-term care. Accidents and many diseases can strike anyone, at any age. Such events don't just affect one person; his or her whole family is affected. Even setting aside tragic events, most people will need long-term care at some point in their lives. That point is difficult to predict since some people age faster than others.

Regardless of the age at which it is needed, long-term care is the most significant financial burden older Americans face. It's not unusual for a nursing home in the Boston area today to charge $120,000 a year. Home care can cost even more.

A colleague of mine has been helping a sick relative struggling with Alzheimer's disease. He was surprised to learn that Medicare did not cover nursing home costs. Another colleague endured a lengthy divorce and custody battle while caring for her sick child. Needless to say, the time involved—and the stress—was considerable, partly because her husband was asserting a claim to her parent's home in which she owned a share. Each suffered employment consequences as a result, and one ultimately declared bankruptcy. Better planning could have made it easier for each of them by protecting certain assets against the risk of high, long-term-care expenses.

The Limited Value of Medicare and Medicaid

MEDICARE

Medicare was established by the government to cover some expenses for a limited time during disability or old age. Medicare pays less than 25 percent of long-term-care costs in the United States. Private insurance often pays for even less. (That's why it's important to carefully scrutinize a long-term-care policy.)

> **DEFINITION MEDICARE**: government plan that provides limited medical coverage during disability or old age

Medicare covers many hospital (Part A), medical (Part B), and prescription drug (Part D) costs. (Medicare Part C is an option to obtain Medicare benefits through a private insurer.) While the benefits Medicare does provide are critical to many seniors in the United States, Medicare does not provide complete coverage. Indeed, it provides very limited coverage for long-term care.

If you have to enter a long-term-care facility, Medicare will likely cover the first twenty days. The next eighty days will be partially covered, with a copay. After the hundredth day, you're on your own as far as the long-term-care facility goes, and that commonly costs around $360 per day, or $11,000 per month. Unfortunately, for this reason, most people must pay out of their own pockets for long-term care—at least until they have depleted their assets enough to be eligible for Medicaid (known as MassHealth in Massachusetts).

MEDICAID

Medicaid was established by the government to cover long-term care for the elderly, disabled, and children—but only if they qualify financially. Many middle-class senior citizens turn to Medicaid to pay for their nursing and healthcare. But there are very strict guidelines on who qualifies, and seniors can't simply offload their assets to lower their estate value because a five-year look-back period applies, to prevent people from doing exactly that in order to qualify for Medicaid. If a disabled person or senior citizen has not planned properly—at least five years in advance—he or she could lose his or her estate to health- and nursing-care costs if they are deemed ineligible for Medicaid.

> **DEFINITION MEDICAID**: government plans that covers long-term medical care for the elderly, disabled, or children who qualify financially

Although the federal government outlines the basic structure of Medicaid, it is administered by state governments. That means each state applies its own rules, and eligibility varies from state to state. Because there are many nuances to this important option, it is discussed in its own section at the end of this chapter.

LONG-TERM-CARE INSURANCE

Deciding whether to purchase long-term-care insurance and choosing which policy to buy are very personal decisions. In addition to the fact that Medicare and Medicaid offer only limited assistance, there are several factors to consider, including affordability, scope of coverage, family history, and, of course, age and eligibility. One thing worth noting is that Massachusetts does not, as of this writing, try to recover MassHealth expenses from the estates of people who own a long-term-care insurance policy approved by the state at the time they enter a nursing home, if the policy provides coverage for at least two years of nursing-home care (at $125 per day or more). Weighing these considerations is beyond the scope of this book, but I urge you to meet with a trusted advisor to assess your long-term-care insurance options.

> **DEFINITION ANNUITY: a financial product that grows while being funded and provides a regular stream of payouts at a later date**

ANNUITIES

An annuity is a contractual financial product sold by financial institutions whereby the institution accepts and grow funds from an individual and then, upon annuitization, provides a stream of payments to the individual at a later point in time. The period of time when an annuity is being funded and before payouts begin is referred to as the accumulation phase.

Once payments start, the contract is in the annuitization phase; this is the period when payouts are being made from an annuity. Annuity payments may be for the life of the annuitant, for a specific number of years, or a combination of the two (for life, but with the guarantee of a certain number of payments even if the annuitant dies prematurely).

Deferred, or variable, annuities are generally considered countable assets that factor into MassHealth eligibility, but immediate annuities are not. Immediate annuities are contracts with insurance companies wherein the annuitant pays a certain sum to the company in exchange for a promise that the company will pay back a fixed monthly amount. Buying an immediate annuity or converting a deferred annuity to an immediate annuity is not treated as a transfer of assets for eligibility purposes if certain requirements are met.

For example, say Harry and Wendy are a married couple in Newton, MA, with $250,000 of countable assets when Harry moves to a nursing home. Wendy could convert $150,000 to an immediate annuity, guaranteeing her a lifetime income stream, at which point Harry would immediately qualify for MassHealth coverage.

A single person in a nursing home with $100,000 in countable assets could also convert it into an income stream with a guaranteed payment of, say, five years. The monthly payments would have to be paid toward the cost of care, but if he or she died before the expiration of the five-year term, the balance of payments would go to any children (or whoever else was named to receive them).

FACT! An immediate annuity can be used to shelter assets for spouses of nursing-home residents and, in some cases, for single individuals.

Note, however, that the guaranteed annuity payments would first go to the state to reimburse it for costs of care paid on behalf of the annuitant. If there are any payments remaining after the state is reimbursed, they can be distributed to family members. Annuities therefore carry an unavoidable risk that the annuitant will pass away before receiving many payments, with the remaining payments going to the state.

MEDICAID AND MASSHEALTH

If you don't have long-term-care insurance, then nursing-home care is generally paid out of pocket. There are advantages to paying privately for nursing-home care, especially if you are trying to enter a particular high-quality facility. But the expense is considerable—in some cases as high as $12,000 per month. Without proper planning, nursing-home residents can easily lose the bulk of their savings to long-term-care expenses.

Those who qualify for MassHealth (or, in other states, Medicaid) may have the alternative option of having some of their nursing-home care covered by MassHealth. MassHealth will look at your countable assets to determine your eligibility. If you are eligible, MassHealth will pay up to $310 per day of your long-term-care costs. But to be eligible, you must be "impoverished" as defined by the strict laws governing MassHealth.

"Impoverished" is a bit of a strong word; you can actually own a home worth $828,000 and still qualify. So you don't have to be completely destitute or even lose your home to receive government assistance. The three biggest problem areas are penalties for transferring assets, home equity, and annuities.

The primary objective of long-term-care planning is to protect your savings for you and your family. Helping you qualify for MassHealth nursing-home benefits may be the best way of doing that. To know for sure, we must consider the MassHealth eligibility rules and the status of your income and your assets under those rules. Some types of assets "count" and others are "exempt," meaning that they are ignored when determining eligibility.

MassHealth Treatment of Assets

EXEMPT ASSETS

To be eligible for MassHealth, you can't have more than $2,000 in "countable" assets in your own name. Countable assets basically include everything except for the following exempt assets:

1. Personal possessions, such as clothing, furniture, and jewelry
2. Your principal Massachusetts residence with up to $828,000 in equity
3. One vehicle, if used for you or your spouse
4. A designated funeral fund (up to $1,500) for you or a prepaid funeral fund (typically limited to about $9,000)

5. A life insurance policy worth up to $1,500
6. Other assets considered inaccessible under the law

MassHealth covers the care of nursing-home residents whose nonexempt assets are below the limits set by the state. In Massachusetts, that limit is currently $2,000 for a nursing-home resident, and $119,220 for his or her spouse. This spousal exemption is called the community spouse resource allowance (CSRA) and is intended to prevent the spouse living at home from becoming impoverished as a consequence of his or her spouse's long-term-care needs.

Asset Transfers

There are strict rules limiting the ability of nursing-home residents to transfer their assets in order to qualify for MassHealth. Some asset transfers can trigger a period of ineligibility based on the state's average private-pay cost of nursing-home care. In Massachusetts, for instance, the penalty is one month of ineligibility for every $9,300 given away, or one day for every $310. A gift of $93,000 would result in ten months of ineligibility (plus taxes payable from the estate). If you expect to enter a nursing home in 2017, and you gave $31,000 to a grandchild for college in 2014, you will have a penalty period of one hundred days. Those one hundred days can easily cost you over $30,000 out of pocket.

KEY PRINCIPLE: If you want to transfer assets in order to be eligible for MassHealth, plan to transfer them five years before you expect to need MassHealth.

Many transfers must be reported on an application for benefits. An applicant must report all transfers made within the five years leading up to the application filing date. (The total length of the ineligibility period depends on the amount transferred.)

The upshot is that anyone transferring assets should assume they won't be eligible for MassHealth for the following five years. That being said, there are certain exceptions that can be helpful. In particular, a transfer of assets to the following people is considered exempt from the transfer penalty:

1. A spouse
2. A blind or disabled child
3. A trust for the benefit of a blind or disabled child
4. A trust for the benefit of a disabled individual under the age of sixty-five

YOUR HOUSE

Up to certain limits, a nursing-home resident's home is not counted against the asset limit for MassHealth eligibility so long as the resident intends to return home. (Although this sounds paradoxical, "intent" is actually simple to establish.) The default limit on excluding the home as a countable asset is $500,000 of home equity. Some states, including Massachusetts, have exercised an option to increase that limit. In Massachusetts, the limit is currently $828,000. Notably, the limit is not applicable so long as a spouse, minor child, or disabled child of the nursing-home resident is living in the house.

For these reasons, MassHealth eligibility is an immediate concern to unmarried nursing-home residents who own a home. Many nursing-home residents do not have to sell their homes to qualify for MassHealth, but if the home is sold, the proceeds are not protected. Furthermore, under certain circumstances, MassHealth will put a lien on the property that entitles it to reimbursement upon sale. Finally, if the house remains in the MassHealth beneficiary's probate estate, it will be subject to estate recovery.

For example, a nursing-home resident who owns an $800,000 home has a $50,000 "countable" asset, and will be ineligible for MassHealth coverage. In this situation, there are a few options:

1. Sell the house and spend the proceeds.
2. Borrow $50,000 against the house to lower the equity to $750,000.
3. Use a lower appraisal to argue that the valuation is wrong. Massachusetts will accept a tax valuation, but you may try to show that the actual market value is lower than the tax assessment.
4. Work out a deal with the nursing home whereby the facility will provide $50,000 of care in exchange for a mortgage on the property.

Special rules apply with respect to the transfer of a home. In addition to being able to make the transfers without penalty to one's spouse, or blind or disabled child, or into trust for other disabled beneficiaries, the applicant may transfer his or her home (or an interest therein) to the following:

1. A child under age twenty-one
2. A sibling who has lived in the home during the year preceding the applicant's institutionalization and who already holds an equity interest in the home
3. A "caretaker child," defined as a child of the applicant who lived in the house for at least two years prior to the applicant's institutionalization, and who, during that period, provided such care that the applicant did not need to move to a nursing home

Finally, a nonexempt transfer can be "cured" by the return of the transferred asset, either partially or in its entirety. In other words, if a mother gives $100,000 to her son, but within five years needs nursing-home care, the son can transfer back the funds. Then, she can spend the money, apply for MassHealth coverage, and be evaluated for eligibility as if she had never made the initial transfer.

MassHealth Treatment of Income

When a nursing-home resident becomes eligible for MassHealth, all of his or her income, less certain deductions, is paid to the nursing home. There is a small personal needs allowance (currently $72.80) and a deduction for any uncovered medical costs (including medical insurance premiums). As you will see below, the situation is different if the nursing-home resident is married with a spouse still living at home.

YOUR SPOUSE: INCOME PROTECTION FOR MARRIED COUPLES

The situation is more favorable if you are married. A married applicant, whose spouse continues to live in their home, may have an exempt portion of their income paid to their spouse. In this situation, the spouse who continues to live at home is called the community spouse. The community spouse is permitted to accept income each month called the monthly maintenance needs allowance (MMNA). The MMNA is between $1,991.25 and $2,980.50 per month (depending on whether a hardship can be demonstrated).

An example will help explain how this works. Let's say Harry and Wendy are married senior citizens, and Wendy has to move into a nursing home. And let's assume Wendy and Harry are collecting the following in Social Security income: Harry gets $1,400 each month, and Wendy gets $1,600 each month. Wendy's $1,600 Social Security check would get distributed as follows:

	Single	Married
Wendy's Social Security Income	$1,600	$1,600
Wendy Keeps	($72.80)	(72.80)
Harry Gets (MMNA)	N/A	($1,527.20)
Nursing Home Gets	($1,527.20)	($0.00)

Keep in mind that there is no limit on the spouse's income, nor is there any obligation that they will contribute any income to the nursing-home resident's spouse's cost of care. There are other potentially applicable exemptions (e.g., for business property) that, depending up on your individual circumstances, may be worth discussing with counsel.

Summary Table: Income and Assets as Categorized Under MassHealth			
		Income	
Countable	Exempt	Community Spouse Exempt	Institutionalized Spouse Countable
Bank Deposits (Savings, Checking, Money Market, CDs)	House (up to $828,000)	Spouse's Assets under CSRA (up to $119,220)	Income (minus $72.80 personal needs allowance)
IRA	One Vehicle	MMNA ($1,991.25/mo to $2,980.50/mo)	Pension
Annuities	Funeral		Social Security
Assets over $2,000	$1,500 in Life Insurance		VA Benefits
	Immediate Annuity		
	Furniture and Personal Items		

Irrevocable Trust Options for Long-Term Care

INCOME-ONLY IRREVOCABLE TRUST

An income-only irrevocable trust has several benefits for those who are able to take advantage of them. If it's properly arranged to meet MassHealth's strict guidelines, assets can be protected, and MassHealth benefits can be used to pay nursing and disability care. You can even transfer an interest in your home to the trust, which can prevent MassHealth from touching it upon your death under its estate-recovery policy. But because assets transferred into this kind of trust will be evaluated using the five-year look-back rule, not everyone has planned far enough in advance to set this up. If you have planned ahead so a proper income-only irrevocable trust can be arranged, you can be assured that your assets will be protected. When the time comes, your beneficiaries will receive them according to your wishes. You'll also be able to draw income from the trust to support your living expenses while Medicaid covers your care.

TESTAMENTARY TRUSTS

Medicaid and MassHealth permit married couples to use a testamentary trust to protect each other from a situation in which one passes away and the other needs nursing-home care. This tool requires a will (and therefore probate) and must be arranged while they are both alive and competent.

The way a testamentary trust works is fairly simple. The estate of the first spouse to pass away goes into trust for the surviving spouse. The trustee (typically one of the couple's children) has total discretion to spend money for the surviving spouse. The trust is funded by money flowing into it from the estate at the end of the probate process. (It's true that, as a general rule, it is preferable to avoid probate, but this is a potential exception.) The funds in the trust are not counted in determining eligibility for MassHealth or Medicaid coverage. In many cases, this plan is less expensive than long-term-care insurance and does not tie up property as an irrevocable trust would. Notably, this remains true even if the surviving spouse moves to another state.

Of course, there are trade-offs, the main one being lack of control. The child cannot control the distributions from the trust and still get the protection the trusts are designed to provide. However, the child may be given some aspects of control over the trust and still maintain some protection. The amount of protection is somewhat uncertain based on recent cases attacking asset-protection trusts. The laws governing this vary from state to state, but the general rule is that the less control the child has, the more ironclad the protection will be.

Summary

Everyone's situation and priorities are different, so there is no one-size-fits-all approach to long-term-care planning. You should, therefore, discuss all of this with a trusted financial advisor. When you do, use the following as a basic checklist:

1. Should I purchase long-term-care insurance? And, if so, will that eliminate the need to consider MassHealth coverage?
2. Should I purchase life insurance through an irrevocable trust? (This would ensure that an inheritance goes to your children, so you can feel comfortable spending down your savings and home equity for your care when and if needed.)
3. Should I file a homestead declaration and put my home in an irrevocable trust? (This is generally advisable, especially if the equity exceeds the state limit, which is $828,000 in Massachusetts. It helps you qualify for Medicaid or MassHealth and protects your home from estate recovery at your death. If your other

resources are insufficient to pay for care during the resulting five-year-penalty period, you may be able to buy long-term-care insurance to cover that period of risk.)

Again, you should consult an elder-law attorney or financial advisor to devise a plan that works for you. When you do so, you can point to this chapter and the table below to ensure that you cover all the correct legal documents and options in creating an estate-planning portfolio.

The Complete Estate-Planning Portfolio

An estate-planning portfolio includes important information that will help you and your family manage your estate and affairs. The following table outlines important components of an estate-planning portfolio.

Revocable Living Trust	With a revocable living trust, your family will avoid living probate and death probate, and can reduce or completely avoid state and federal estate taxes.
Divorce Protection Trust	To ensure that the estate you spent a lifetime building passes to family in your bloodline, a divorce protection trust is put in place in the event that your children and/or beneficiaries go through a divorce.
Trust Property	This is simply a list of all the assets owned by the living trust.

Pour-Over Will	A pour-over will ensures that upon your death, any assets you still hold outside of the living trust are transferred into the trust so they can be subject to your wishes as specified in the trust.
Certificate of Trust	This is a summary of the most important sections of the trust.
Funding Letters	When you transfer assets into your living trust, related financial institutions must be informed in writing. Copies of these letters are included in the trust.
Location List for Family	When you become sick or have passed away, your family will need to know where all of your important documents are kept. This is a list of those documents and their locations.
Notification Information	This is a list of people who should be notified in the event of your incapacitation or death.
Planning Letter	This letter outlines your instructions for how your funeral and burial should be carried out. It also lists the distribution of personal items that have sentimental value, such as family heirlooms, photographs, and so on.

Durable Power of Attorney	If you become unable to manage your affairs due to mental or physical disability, you can give power of attorney to someone you trust so they can manage your estate and make decisions on your behalf.
Healthcare Proxy	Your living trust can stipulate who is authorized to make healthcare decisions if you are incapacitated.
Living Will	If you have a terminal illness that you're not expected to recover from, your living trust can stipulate that life support be terminated.
HIPAA Authorization	In order for your healthcare proxy to make informed medical decisions, they must have access to your medical records. The HIPAA authorization gives your approval for your records to be shared with them.

Conclusion

Asset protection planning is extremely important to seniors because most do not have the option of going back to work. The biggest threat to the financial security for most seniors is disability and the need for long-term care.

Planning for this risk is critical. Healthcare costs can be paid via savings and earnings, long-term-care insurance, MassHealth, or some combination of the three. To protect your nest egg responsibly, you must plan ahead—not only by saving and investing wisely but also by making sure you have the right legal documents in place. There are a lot of moving parts to this type of planning, but a trusted advisor can help your navigate it. Such an investment of time and resources is well worth it.

About David E. Rosen, Esq.

I founded the Rosen Law Group in 2012 to help people plan their estates with minimal hassle and maximum asset protection. I founded Rosen Investment Management, a registered investment-advisory firm, in 2013. I had seen too many hardworking people without a retirement plan and with investment portfolios that not only made no sense but also were actually hurting them. I want my clients to have peace of mind in the years leading up to their retirement and be able to enjoy it, secure in the knowledge that they have protected their family's best interests after their passing. To that end, I frequently teach workshops on estate planning, nursing-home-asset protection, and retirement planning.

Good financial advice should be tailored to you, and your financial plan should be *coordinated* with your estate plan. We take a holistic approach to providing coordinated estate planning, retirement planning, and investment management. The estate plan is designed to protect your assets from taxes, probate fees, and nursing homes.

As a registered investment advisor, I hold a Series 65 license from the North American Securities Administrators Association, so Rosen Investment Management (namely me) can act as your fiduciary to ensure your portfolio is working for you.

If you are in the Boston or Newton, Massachusetts area, please call to set up a free consultation. We will address all of your needs, hopes, and concerns: Will you run out of money? Will you be able to maintain your lifestyle? How can you avoid becoming a burden on your loved ones?

After taking stock of your situation, we will structure a unique, personalized game plan for how Rosen Law Group and/or Rosen Investment Management can help you prepare for the future. Please contact us for further information.

Definition of Terms and Acronyms

12b-1 fee. An annual marketing or distribution fee on a mutual fund, named for the section of the Investment Company Act of 1940.

asset. An economic resource; it can be tangible (like cash, inventory, or equipment) or intangible (like copyrights, patents, stocks, and bonds).

accumulation phase. The period when the annuity is being funded but payouts have not begun.

annuitization. The period when payouts are being made from an annuity.

annuity. Financial product that grows while being funded and provides a regular stream of payouts at a later date.

bid/ask spread. The difference between what the broker paid you for the stock and what he sells the stock for to the next buyer.

blue chip. Nationally recognized, financially sound companies. They are stable, and their growth tends to mirror that of the S&P 500.

cap-weight. A type of market index whose individual components are weighted according to their market capitalization so that larger components carry a larger percentage weighting.

CFA. Certified financial analyst.

CFO. Chief financial officer.

correlation. A connection or relationship between two or more things. Investments that are positively correlated will be affected by the same systematic risk, such as a slowdown in manufacturing in Japan. Investments that are negatively correlated will not be affected by the same conditions, and their prices won't respond in the same way.

CRSP. Center for Research in Security Prices.

death plan. A court process used to distribute your estate after your death.

estate plan. A legally binding plan that defines how your wealth will be managed if you need to be cared for in sickness, plus how your wealth will be distributed after your death.

ETF. Exchange-traded funds.

FAQ. Frequently asked questions.

fiduciary duty. A legal requirement to act in the best interests of another party.

financial benchmark. A standard against which the performance of a stock, bond, mutual fund, or any other financial instrument can be measured.

FINRA. Financial Industry Regulatory Authority.

fixed income. Investments (typically municipal bonds or Treasuries) that pay a predictable premium on a regular schedule.

healthcare proxy. Designates the power to make medical decisions on your behalf to someone you designate.

HIPAA. Healthcare Insurance Portability and Accountability Act.

homestead declaration. Protects up to $500,000 of equity in your home from creditors (limits vary by state).

IRA. Individual retirement account.

IRS. Internal Revenue Service.

joint tenancy. Shared ownership of a property by two or more people avoids probate by having the property pass to other joint tenants upon death of one.

living probate. A court process that determines how your estate is to be managed so your medical and nursing-home-care bills can be paid if you are incapacitated.

living trust. Holds title to your assets to protect your estate from probate.

longevity risk. The risk that you will outlive your assets.

MassHealth. State of Massachusetts healthcare coverage for Massachusetts residents unable to afford their own care.

Medicare. Government plan that provides limited medical coverage during disability or old age.

Medicaid. Government plans that covers long-term medical care for the elderly, disabled, or children who qualify financially.

MMNA. Monthly maintenance needs allowance.

mutual fund. A pool of funds collected from many investors for the purpose of investing in securities such as stocks, bonds, money-market instruments, and similar assets.

NYSE. New York Stock Exchange.

opportunity cost. A determination of gain forgone when funds are used for an alternate purpose. For example, the cost of attending business school is not only the expense of tuition but also the salary not earned during that two-year period.

POA. Power of attorney.

probability theory. The analysis of random phenomena. It is not possible to predict the outcome of discrete events.

probate. A legal process that pays debts owed by your estate and applicable death taxes and distributes the remainder of your estate to your designated beneficiaries.

risk tolerance. Your personal willingness to lose some or all of your investment capital in exchange for larger potential returns.

sales load. A sales charge or commission that's charged to an investor when buying or redeeming shares in a mutual fund.

SEC. Securities and Exchange Commission.

S&P 500 index. The S&P 500 is a US stock market index based on the market capitalization of five hundred large companies listed on the New York Stock Exchange **(NYSE)** or **NASDAQ.** It is a representation of the US stock market.

systematic risk. The risk inherent to the entire market or market segment.

systemic risk. An event that can trigger a collapse in a certain industry or economy.

time horizon. The anticipated amount of time you expect to invest in order to achieve a specific goal.

transaction cost. Fees or commissions paid when buying or selling an investment.

turnover ratio. The percentage of the fund's holdings that have been sold and replaced with other holdings during the course of the year.

unsystematic risk. Company- or industry-specific hazard that is inherent in each investment.

Notes

i   In fact, studies indicate that many of Jim Cramer's recommendations on his CNBC show *Mad Money* lead to lousy returns in the long run. Joseph Engelberg, Caroline Sasseville, and Jared Williams, *Market Madness? The Case of Mad Money* (October 20, 2010): http://papers.ssrn.com/sol3/papers.cfm?abstract_id=870498. More specifically, they show that Cramer's recommendations are hot at the time he recommends them, and they continue to be hot for a short time thereafter, at which point the stock prices return to reality. It's herd-based investing—Cramer's recommendation gets more people to run with the crowd. It makes me think of a flock of birds in the sky, scrambling to follow the leader.

ii   https://web.archive.org/web/20160219234859/http://www.un-museum.or g/lightbulb.htm.

iii   I like to keep it simple by focusing on what I consider to be the four myths that tend to cause the biggest problems. But there are many other myths out there. See, for example, Daniel Solin, "5 Investment Myths That Can Cost You," *US News and World Report* (March 17, 2011): https://web.archive.org/web/20160220002839/http://www.businessinsid er.com/5-common-investing-myths-that-could-cost-you-money-2014-9.

iv   Jeff Somer, "Who Routinely Trounces the Market? Try 2 Out of 2,862 Funds," *New York Times* (July 19, 2014): https://web.archive.org/web/20160219235323/http://www.nytimes.com/2014/07/20/your-money/who-routinely-trounces-the-stock-market-try- 2-out-of-2862-funds.html.

v   Sometimes people want to hold so many shares of a particular stock, not out of greed or fear of missing out but because they or someone they love worked for a company with which they have an emotional attachment. If you are adamant about doing that with respect to one or two stocks, and it makes up only a tiny fraction of your portfolio, you can do it. If you do it on your own, be sure to inform your investment advisor representative. Or you can do it through your advisor, who will probably tell you not to speculate and make you sign a waiver.

vi   This chart from Chartsource, published by S&P Capital IQ Financial Communications, is provided solely to illustrate the difference between growth of a $10,000 initial investment in the S&P 500 if invested continuously for the entire period versus missing the market's top performing days during the same period. It is believed, but not guaranteed, to be accurate. The S&P 500 index, described in the endnotes, is unmanaged and cannot be invested in directly. Its returns do not represent the performance of any actual fund or transactions and do not include management fees and transaction costs or expenses. Past performance is no guarantee of future success.

vii Another thing to keep in mind is that, in practice, this is a nuanced speculation process, and fund managers sitting on mountains of money are able to spread their bets over time—for instance, if they are very confident there's going to be a spike, they could be right yet get the timing wrong. So on week one they think something has hit bottom, but they are not sure. They have set aside a pot of money to make this bet. They invest, say, 20 percent on week one, knowing they probably don't have the timing exactly right but not wanting to miss out in case they are right. If the stock continues to dive in week two, but nothing else really changes, they can double down on their bet—investing say 25 percent in week two at the lower price. If they are wrong in week two but still confident, they may bet 30 percent of their pot on week three at an even lower price. If the stock rebounds strongly in week four, the manager looks like a genius. If not, they just lost a lot of money. If that sounds to you more like a guy at the craps table in Vegas than one practicing sound investment strategies, you're right!

viii https://web.archive.org/web/20160219235603/http://www.investopedia.com/terms/e/efficientmarke thypothesis.asp.

ix The company was officially founded the following year. In January 2015, it reported the biggest quarterly profit in corporate history (Q4 2014).

xi Each category in the table is an index used by Dalbar. The indices do not represent the performance of any actual fund, and they do not include management fees, transaction costs, or expenses. Dalbar defines the "average investor" to include all mutual-fund investors whose actions and financial results are restated to represent a single investor.

xi Sam Mamudi, "Investors Caught With Stars in Their Eyes," *Wall Street Journal* (June 1, 2010): http://www.wsj.com/articles/SB100 01424052748703957604575272246184 0998720.

xiii Ferri, Richard. "Any Monkey Can Beat the Market," *Forbes* (December 20, 2012):http://www.forbes.com/sites/rickferri/2012/12/20/any-monkey-can-beat-the-market/#5f95c7b56e8b.

xiv   Fama and French define "value" companies as those in the bottom 30 percent of all companies listed on the NYSE.

xv   A controversial fee that is supposed to be included in the expense ratio as an operational expense is the 12B-1 fee, which gets its name from a section of the Investment Company Act of 1940. It typically totals 0.25 percent to 1.0 percent (the maximum allowed by law) of a fund's net assets and covers marketing or distribution costs.

xvi   "Mutual Fund Expense Ratio Trends" (June 2014): https://web. archive.org/web/20160220001810/https://corporate.morningstar.com/US/documents/researchpapers/Fee_Trend.pdf.

xvii   Brett Carson, "The Mutual Fund Fees We Don't Talk About," *US News and World Report: The Smarter Investor* (blog) (March 4, 2015): https://web.archive.org/web/20160220001922/http://money.usnews.com/money/blogs/the-smarter-mutual-fund-investor/2015/03/04/the-mutual-fund-fees-we-dont-talk-about.

xviii   "Why Even Experienced Fund Managers Don't Beat the Market," *Business Insider* (August 10, 2014): https://web.archive.org/web/20160220003408/http://www.businessinsid er.com/why-even-experienced-fund-managers-dont-beat-the-market- 2014-8.

xix   Roger M. Eldelan, Richard B. Evans, and Gregory B. Kadlec, "Scale Effects in Mutual Fund Performance: The Role of Trading Costs" (March 17, 2007): https://web.archive.org/web/20160220003625/http://www.frontieradvis orsllc.com/files/1267653327_The%20Role%20of%20Trading%20Costs%20in%20MFs.pdf.

xx   See 15 USC § 80b-5 (2015); 17 C.F.R. § 275.205-3 (SEC Rule 205-3).

xxi   See Stephen M. Schultz, "Performance Based Fees Under the Investment Advisers Act of 1940," *The Business Lawyer* 39 (1984): 521, https://web.archive.org/web/20160220004554/ https://www.sec.gov/rules /final/2012/ia-3372.pdf.

xxii   Jason Karceski, Miles Livingston, and Edward O'Neal, "Mutual Fund Brokerage Commissions" (January 2004): http://citeseerx. ist.psu.edu/viewdoc/download?doi=10.1.1.167.6016&rep=rep1&t ype=pdf.

xxiii   Stephen M. Horan and D. Bruce Johnsen. "Does Soft Dollar Brokerage Benefit Portfolio Investors: Agency Problem or Solution?" (George Mason University School of Law:2004): https://web.archive.org/web/20160220004449/http://papers. ssrn.com/sol 3/papers.cfm?abstract_id=615281.

xxiv   "Deciphering Funds' Hidden Costs." *Wall Street Journal* (March 17, 2004): https://web.archive.org/web/20160220004341/http:// www.wsj.com/articles/SB107948739963057538.

xxv   There are "closed end" mutual funds that sell a fixed number of shares at an initial public offering (IPO) and do not offer new shares for sale thereafter. Because they tend to be sector-specific, highly speculative, and actively managed, they are outside the scope of this book.

xxvi   What qualifies as "small" or "large," you ask? Well, one rule of thumb is to define small companies as those with under $1 billion in market capitalization. A more refined way is to rank all publicly traded companies by the size of their market capitalization and call the largest 20 percent "large" and the smallest 20 percent "small." The University of Chicago Center for Research in Security Prices provides a database that helps managers do that.

xxvii Book value refers to total assets minus total liabilities. If a company's stock is not worth much more than its book value, it's in distress.

xxviii Fama and French define "value" companies as those in the bottom 30 percent of all companies listed on the NYSE.

xxix Mark M. Carhart, "On Persistence in Mutual Fund Performance," *Journal of Finance*, 52, no. 1, (March 1997): 57–82 (estimating that turnover reduces performance about 0.95 percent for each buy-and-sell transaction), https://web.archive.org/web/20160220174833/http://faculty.chicagoboot h.edu/john.cochrane/teaching/35150_advanced_investments/Carhart_f unds_jf.pdf.

xxx Gary P. Brinson, L. Randolf Hood, and Gilbert L. Beebower, "Determinants of Portfolio Performance," *Financial Analysts Journal*, (1986, 1990, 1991): http://dx.doi.org/10.2469/faj.v42.n4.39.

xxxi The government has recently proposed changing this rule to better protect investors, but as of this writing, no such change in the law has been finalized.

xxxii "The Human Touch: The Role of Financial Advisors in a Changing Advice Landscape" (October 13, 2015): https://web.archive.org/web/20160220174507/https://corp.financialengi nes.com/research/FE-The-Role-of-Financial-Advisors-1015.pdf.

xxxiii Some advisors are also registered with the Securities and Exchange Commission, and their registration information can be found on the SEC's investment-advisor public-disclosure page: www.advisorinfo.sec.gov.

xxxiv It bears noting that for many investors, the fee paid to a registered investment advisor may be tax deductible, whereas the brokerage fees or commissions paid to brokers are not.

xxxv Estate taxes in general and the Massachusetts estate tax, in particular, are discussed further in chapter 12.

xxxvi This unlimited marital deduction applies only if the surviving spouse is a US citizen. If not, entirely different rules apply.

xxxvii See Ed Slott, CPA, *The Retirement Tax Bomb…and How to Defuse It*, 2008.

xxxviii You may have heard of the unified tax credit. This was repealed in 2010. Instead, as of 2015, there is a basic exclusion amount of $5.43 million. Generally, if the total of the taxable estate and lifetime gifts is under that threshold, there is no federal estate tax obligation.

xxxix For purposes of determining whether an estate is taxable, prior taxable gifts (over $14,000) are included in the value of the estate. Such gifts do not factor into the actual calculation of the tax, however.

xl "Risks and Process of Retirement Survey Report," Society of Actuaries (2012).

Made in the USA
San Bernardino, CA
20 July 2016